PRAISE FOR *Running in the Family*

"A fever dream of a book, delirious, saturated with colour; it's a travel book, and a family history, and a memoir, and it's funny and unforgettable." Nick Hornby, *The Believer*

"Brief, vivid scenes, moments revived out of remote memories, pictures of the intensities lived by his passionate parents amid the lush flora, the predatory fauna, and the old-fashioned life of the British colonies. This is great storytelling." Leon Edel

"Impossible to put down." *Winnipeg Free Press*

"A brilliant, charming, poetic, hyperbolic holiday of a book." *Vancouver Province*

"A remarkable book. . . . Shimmering through the haze of heat and memory is an impressionistic, sometimes surreal portrait of an exotic time and place now gone, a colonial paradise that had its own rhythms and imperatives." *The Globe and Mail*

"An outstandingly evocative, semi-autobiographical account of a journey back to the beginning, to Ceylon where Ondaatje was born into a privileged group of mixed Dutch, Tamil and Sinhalese origins. Created from asides, snapshots, poems, glimpses in every way unorthodox and incomplete, it falls magically on the page with all the grace of a billowing, seamless dress. Like all classic writing, the motion of this book lingers on, like the movement of a boat, long after the last pages." *New Statesman*

"In the twenty years of my adult book discussion group at the library . . . one title stands out for the sheer delight it occasioned us all—*Running in the Family*." Shyam Selvadurai

"Ondaatje describes Ceylon so completely you feel as though you could actually be with him, walking through the tea fields and napping in the heavy, damp afternoons. His descriptive powers are matched by his observations of human nature."

January Magazine

"Sparkles with the intensity and vividness of its multifaceted tales of romance and intrigue." *Fort Worth Star-Telegram*

"Eloquent, oblique, witty, full of light and feeling. . . . Ondaatje's knowledge of the fragility and luck of life is very clear. So, too, is the grace and originality of his prose." *The New Yorker*

"Dazzles with its range of imagination, richness of language and the consistently evolving changes of mood and tempo."

Toronto Star

"With a prose style equal to the voluptuousness of Ondaatje's subject and a sense of humour never too far away, *Running in the Family* is sheer reading pleasure." *The Washington Post*

"Languid, exquisite, gently humorous."

The New York Review of Books

"Ondaatje's memoir, *Running in the Family*, conjures up fascinating images of his native country, Sri Lanka. The book reads half like a thoughtful memoir, half like a travel guide, describing in flawless detail the lush, rich, and equally dark nature of Sri Lanka's wild forests and hidden avenues. Ondaatje masterfully enhances his prose with touches of magic realism." *World Literature Forum*

"A beautiful, luscious book of discovery and remembrance."

The Hamilton Spectator

ALSO BY MICHAEL ONDAATJE

FICTION
Coming Through Slaughter (1976)
In the Skin of a Lion (1987)
The English Patient (1992)
Anil's Ghost (2000)
Divisadero (2007)
The Cat's Table (2011)

POETRY
The Dainty Monsters (1967)
The Man with Seven Toes (1969)
The Collected Works of Billy the Kid (1970)
Rat Jelly (1973)
Elimination Dance (1976)
There's a Trick with a Knife I'm Learning to Do (1979)
Tin Roof (1982)
Secular Love (1984)
The Cinnamon Peeler (1991)
Handwriting (1998)
The Story (2006)

NON-FICTION
The Conversations: Walter Murch and the Art of Editing Film (2002)

MICHAEL ONDAATJE

—

RUNNING
IN THE
FAMILY

VINTAGE CANADA

VINTAGE CANADA EDITION, 2011

Copyright © 1982 Michael Ondaatje

Published in Canada by Vintage Canada, a division of Random House of Canada Limited, Toronto, in 2011. Originally published in hardcover in Canada by McClelland & Stewart Ltd., in 1982. Distributed by Random House of Canada Limited.

Vintage Canada with colophon is a registered trademark.

www.randomhouse.ca

LIBRARY AND ARCHIVES CANADA CATALOGUING IN PUBLICATION

Ondaatje, Michael, 1943–
Running in the family / Michael Ondaatje.

Issued also in electronic format.

ISBN 978-0-307-40119-9

1. Ondaatje, Michael, 1943–. 2. Authors, Canadian (English)—20th century—Biography. 3. Poets, Canadian (English)—20th century—Biography. 4. Sri Lanka—Biography. I. Title.

PS8529.N283Z47 2011   C818'.5409   C2011-902006-8

Book design by Antonina Krass

Printed and bound in the United States of America

2 4 6 8 9 7 5 3 1

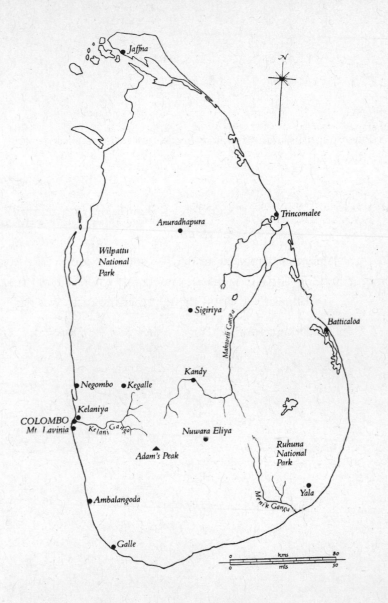

N

Jaffna

Trincomalee

Anuradhapura

Wilpattu
National
Park

Sigiriya

Batticaloa

Mahaweli Ganga

Negombo   Kegalle   Kandy

Kelaniya

COLOMBO
Mt Lavinia   *Kelani Ganga*

Nuwara Eliya

Adam's Peak

Ruhuna
National
Park

Menik Ganga

Yala

Ambalangoda

Galle

0   kms   80
0   mls   50

"I saw in this island fowls as big as our country geese having
two heads . . . and other miraculous things which I will not
here write of."

Oderic (Franciscan Friar, 14th century)

"The Americans were able to put a man on the moon because
they knew English. The Sinhalese and Tamils whose knowledge
of English was poor, thought that the earth was flat."

Douglas Amarasekera, *Ceylon Sunday Times* 29.1.78

CONTENTS

For Griffin and Quintin.
For Gillian, Janet, and Christopher.

RUNNING
IN THE
FAMILY

Drought since December.

All across the city men roll carts with ice clothed in sawdust. Later on, during a fever, the drought still continuing, his nightmare is that thorn trees in the garden send their hard roots underground towards the house climbing through windows so they can drink sweat off his body, steal the last of the saliva off his tongue.

He snaps on the electricity just before daybreak. For twenty five years he has not lived in this country, though up to the age of eleven he slept in rooms like this — with no curtains, just delicate bars across the windows so no one could break in. And the floors of red cement polished smooth, cool against bare feet.

Dawn through a garden. Clarity to leaves, fruit, the dark yellow of the King Coconut. This delicate light is allowed only a brief moment of the day. In ten minutes the garden will lie in a blaze of heat, frantic with noise and butterflies.

Half a page — and the morning is already ancient.

ASIAN
RUMOURS

ASIA

What began it all was the bright bone of a dream I could hardly hold onto. I was sleeping at a friend's house. I saw my father, chaotic, surrounded by dogs, and all of them were screaming and barking into the tropical landscape. The noises woke me. I sat up on the uncomfortable sofa and I was in a jungle, hot, sweating. Street lights bounced off the snow and into the room through the hanging vines and ferns at my friend's window. A fish tank glowed in the corner. I had been weeping and my shoulders and face were exhausted. I wound the quilt around myself, leaned back against the head of the sofa, and sat there for most of the night. Tense, not wanting to move as the heat gradually left me, as the sweat evaporated and I became conscious again of brittle air outside the windows searing and howling through the streets and over the frozen cars hunched like sheep all the way down towards Lake Ontario. It was a new winter and I was already dreaming of Asia.

Once a friend had told me that it was only when I was drunk that I seemed to know exactly what I wanted. And so, two months later, in the midst of the farewell party in my growing wildness — dancing, balancing a wine glass on my forehead and falling to the floor twisting round and getting up without letting the glass tip, a trick which seemed only possible when drunk and relaxed — I knew I was already running. Outside the continuing snow had made the streets narrow, almost impassable. Guests had arrived on foot, scarved, faces pink and frozen. They leaned against the fire-place and drank.

I had already planned the journey back. During quiet afternoons I spread maps onto the floor and searched out possible routes to Ceylon. But it was only in the midst of this party, among my closest friends, that I realized I would be travelling back to the family I had grown from — those relations from my parents' generation who stood in my memory like frozen opera. I wanted to touch them into words. A perverse and solitary desire. In Jane Austen's *Persuasion* I had come across the lines, "she had been forced into prudence in her youth — she learned romance as she grew older — the natural sequence of an unnatural beginning." In my mid-thirties I realized I had slipped past a childhood I had ignored and not understood.

Asia. The name was a gasp from a dying mouth. An ancient word that had to be whispered, would never be used as a battle cry. The word sprawled. It had none of the clipped sound of Europe, America, Canada. The vowels took over, slept on the map with the S. I was running to Asia and everything would change. It began with that moment when I was dancing and laughing wildly within the comfort and order of my life. Beside the fridge

I tried to communicate some of the fragments I knew about my father, my grandmother. "So how *did* your grandmother die?" "Natural causes." "What?" "Floods." And then another wave of the party swirled me away.

JAFFNA AFTERNOONS

2:15 in the afternoon. I sit in
the huge living room of the
old governor's home in Jaffna. The walls, painted in recent years
a warm rose-red, stretch awesome distances away to my left to
my right and up towards a white ceiling. When the Dutch first
built this house egg white was used to paint the walls. The doors
are twenty feet high, as if awaiting the day when a family of acro-
bats will walk from room to room, sideways, without dismantling
themselves from each other's shoulders.

The fan hangs on a long stem, revolves lethargic, its arms in
a tilt to catch the air which it folds across the room. No matter
how mechanical the fan is in its movement the textures of air
have no sense of the metronome. The air reaches me unevenly
with its gusts against my arms, face, and this paper.

The house was built around 1700 and is the prize building in
this northern region of Ceylon. In spite of its internal vastness

it appears modest from the outside, tucked in one corner of the fort. To approach the building by foot or car or bicycle one has to cross a bridge over the moat, be accepted by two sentries who unfortunately have to stand exactly where marsh gases collect, and enter the fort's yard. Here, in this spacious centre of the labyrinth of 18th-century Dutch defense I sit on one of the giant sofas, in the noisy solitude of the afternoon while the rest of the house is asleep.

The morning has been spent with my sister and my Aunt Phyllis trying to trace the maze of relationships in our ancestry. For a while we sat in one of the bedrooms sprawled on two beds and a chair. The twin to this bedroom, in another part of the house, is dark and supposedly haunted. Walking into that room's dampness, I saw the mosquito nets stranded in the air like the dresses of hanged brides, the skeletons of beds without their mattresses, and retreated from the room without ever turning my back on it.

Later the three of us moved to the dining room while my Aunt plucked notorious incidents from her brain. She is the minotaur of this long journey back — all those preparations for travel, the journey through Africa, the recent 7-hour train ride from Colombo to Jaffna, the sentries, the high walls of stone, and now this lazy courtesy of meals, tea, her best brandy in the evenings for my bad stomach — the minotaur who inhabits the place one had been years ago, who surprises one with conversations about the original circle of love. I am especially fond of her because she was always close to my father. When someone else speaks, her eyes glance up to the ceilings of the room, as if noticing the architecture there for the first time, as if looking for the cue cards for stories. We are still recovering from her gleeful résumé of the life and death of one foul Ondaatje who was "savaged to pieces by his own horse."

Eventually we move out onto the wicker chairs of the porch which runs 50 yards along the front of the house. From ten until noon we sit talking and drinking ice-cold palmyra toddy from a bottle we have filled in the village. This is a drink which smells of raw rubber and is the juice drained from the flower of a coconut. We sip it slowly, feeling it continue to ferment in the stomach.

At noon I doze for an hour, then wake for a lunch of crab curry. There is no point in using a fork and spoon for this meal. I eat with my hands, shovelling in the rice with my thumb, crunching the shell in my teeth. Then fresh pineapple.

But I love the afternoon hours most. It is now almost a quarter to three. In half an hour the others will waken from their sleep and intricate conversations will begin again. In the heart of this 250-year-old fort we will trade anecdotes and faint memories, trying to swell them with the order of dates and asides, interlocking them all as if assembling the hull of a ship. No story is ever told just once. Whether a memory or funny hideous scandal, we will return to it an hour later and retell the story with additions and this time a few judgements thrown in. In this way history is organized. All day my Uncle Ned, who is heading a commission on race-riots (and so has been given this building to live in while in Jaffna), is at work, and all day my Aunt Phyllis presides over the history of good and bad Ondaatjes and the people they came in contact with. Her eye, which by now knows well the ceilings of this house, will suddenly sparkle and she will turn to us with delight and begin "and there is another terrible story. . . ."

There are so many ghosts here. In the dark mildewed wing, where the rotting mosquito nets hang, lives the apparition of the Dutch governor's daughter. In 1734 she threw herself down a well after being told she could not marry her lover, and has startled generations since, making them avoid the room where she silently exhibits herself in a red dress. And just as the haunted sections are avoided for sleeping, the living room is avoided for conversation, being so huge that all talk evaporates into the air before it reaches the listener.

The dogs from the town, who have sneaked past the guards, are asleep on the porch — one of the coolest spots in Jaffna. As I get up to adjust the speed of the fan, they roll onto their feet and move a few yards down the porch. The tree outside is full of crows and white cranes who gurgle and screech. A noisy solitude — all the new stories in my mind and the birds totally compatible but screaming at each other, sweeping now and then over the heads of drowsy mongrels.

*　*　*

That night, I will have not so much a dream as an image that repeats itself. I see my own straining body which stands shaped like a star and realize gradually I am part of a human pyramid. Below me are other bodies that I am standing on and above me are several more, though I am quite near the top. With cumbersome slowness we are walking from one end of the huge living room to the other. We are all chattering away like the crows and cranes so that it is often difficult to hear. I do catch one piece of dialogue. A Mr. Hobday has asked my father if he has any Dutch antiques in the house. And he replies, "Well . . . there *is* my mother." My grandmother lower down gives a roar of anger. But at this point we are approaching the door which being twenty feet high we will be able to pass through only if the pyramid turns sideways. Without discussing it the whole family ignores the opening and walks slowly through the pale pink rose-coloured walls into the next room.

A FINE
ROMANCE

THE COURTSHIP

When my father finished school, his parents decided to send him to university in England. So leaving Ceylon by ship Mervyn Ondaatje arrived at Southampton. He took his entrance exams for Cambridge and, writing home a month later, told his parents the good news that he had been accepted at Queen's College. They sent him the funds for three years of university education. Finally he had made good. He had been causing much trouble at home and now seemed to have pulled himself out of that streak of bad behaviour in the tropics.

It was two and a half years later, after several modest letters about his successful academic career, that his parents discovered he had not even passed the entrance exam and was living off their money in England. He had rented extravagant rooms in Cambridge and simply eliminated the academic element of university, making close friends among the students, reading contemporary novels, boating, and making a name for himself as someone who knew exactly what was valuable and interesting in the Cambridge circles of the 1920s. He had a good time, becoming briefly engaged to a Russian countess, even taking a short trip to Ireland supposedly to fight against the Rebels when the university closed down for its vacation. No one knew about this Irish adventure except an aunt who was sent a photograph of him posing slyly in uniform.

On hearing the distressing news, his parents decided to confront him personally, and so his mother and father and sister Stephy packed their trunks and left for England by ship. In any case my father had just twenty-four more days of high living at Cambridge before his furious family arrived unannounced at his doors. Sheepishly he invited them in, being able to offer them only champagne at eleven in the morning. This did not impress them as he had hoped, while the great row which my grandfather had looked forward to for weeks and weeks was deflected by my father's useful habit of retreating into almost total silence, of never trying to justify any of his crimes, so that it was difficult to argue with him. Instead he went out at dinnertime for a few hours and came back to announce that he had become engaged to Kaye Roseleap — his sister Stephy's closest English friend. This news stilled most of the fury against him. Stephy moved onto his side and his parents were impressed by the fact that Kaye leapt from the notable Roseleaps of Dorset. On the whole everybody was pleased and the following day they all caught the train to the country to stay with the Roseleaps, taking along my father's cousin Phyllis.

During the week in Dorset my father behaved impeccably. The in-laws planned the wedding, Phyllis was invited to spend the summer with the Roseleaps, and the Ondaatjes (including my father) went back to Ceylon to wait out the four months before the marriage.

Two weeks after he arrived in Ceylon, my father came home one evening to announce that he was engaged to a Doris Gratiaen. The postponed argument at Cambridge now erupted on my grandfather's lawn in Kegalle. My father was calm and unconcerned with the various complications he seemed to have created and did not even plan to write to the Roseleaps. It was Stephy who wrote, setting off a chain reaction in the mails, one letter going to Phyllis whose holiday plans were terminated. My father continued with his technique of trying to solve one problem by creating another. The next day he returned home saying he had joined the Ceylon Light Infantry.

I am not sure how long he had known my mother before the engagement. He must have met her socially now and then before his Cambridge years, for one of his closest friends was Noel Gratiaen, my mother's brother. About this time, Noel returned to Ceylon, sent down from Oxford at the end of his first year for setting fire to his room. This in fact was common behaviour, but he had gone one step further, trying to put out the fire by throwing flaming sofas and armchairs out of the window onto the street and then dragging and hurling them into the river — where they sank three boats belonging to the Oxford rowing team. It was probably while visiting Noel in Colombo that my father first met Doris Gratiaen.

At that time Doris Gratiaen and Dorothy Clementi-Smith would perform radical dances in private, practising daily. Both women were about twenty-two and were greatly influenced by rumours of the dancing of Isadora Duncan. In a year or so they would perform in public. There is a reference to them in Rex Daniels' journals:

A garden party at the Residency Grounds. . . . Bertha and I sat next to the Governor and Lady Thompson. A show had been organized for them made up of various acts. First on was a ventriloquist from Trincomalee whose act was not vetted as he had arrived late. He was drunk and began to tell insulting jokes about the Governor. The act was stopped and was followed by Doris Gratiaen and Dorothy Clementi-Smith who did an item called "Dancing Brass Figures". They wore swimsuits and had covered themselves in gold metallic paint. It was a very beautiful dance but the gold paint had an allergic effect on the girls and the next day they were covered in a terrible red rash.

My father first saw them dance in the gardens of Deal Place. He would drive down from his parents' home in Kegalle to Colombo, stay at the Ceylon Light Infantry quarters, and spend his days with Noel watching the two girls practise. It is said he was enchanted with *both* girls, but Noel married Dorothy while my father became engaged to Noel's sister. More to keep my father company than anything else, Noel too had joined the Ceylon Light Infantry. This engagement of my father's was not as popular as the Roseleap one. He bought Doris Gratiaen a huge emerald engagement ring which he charged to his father's account. His father refused to pay and my father threatened to shoot himself. Eventually it was paid for by the family.

My father had nothing to do in Kegalle. It was too far away from Colombo and his new friends. His position with the Light Infantry was a casual one, almost a hobby. Often, in the midst of a party in Colombo, he would suddenly remember he was the duty officer that night and with a car full of men and women planning a midnight swim at Mount Lavinia, he would roll into the barracks, step out in his dress suit, inspect the guard, leap back into the car full of laughing and drunken friends and depart. But in Kegalle he was frustrated and lonely. Once he was given the car and asked to go and buy some fish. *Don't* forget the fish! his mother said. Two days later his parents got a telegram from Trincomalee, miles away in the north end of the island, to say he had the fish and would be back soon.

His quiet life in Kegalle was interrupted, however, when Doris Gratiaen wrote to break off the engagement. There were no phones, so it meant a drive to Colombo to discover what was wrong. But my grandfather, furious over the Trincomalee trip, refused him the car. Finally he got a lift with his father's brother Aelian. Aelian was a gracious and genial man and my father was bored and frantic. The combination almost proved disastrous. My father had never driven to Colombo directly in his life. There was a pattern of rest-houses to be stopped at and so Aelian was forced to stop every ten miles and have a drink, too polite to refuse his young nephew. By the time they got to Colombo my father was very drunk and Aelian was slightly drunk and it was too late to visit Doris Gratiaen anyway. My father forced his Uncle to stay at the CLI mess. After a large meal and more drink my father announced that now he must shoot himself because Doris had broken off the engagement. Aelian, especially as he was quite drunk too, had a terrible time trying to hide every gun in the Ceylon Light Infantry building. The next day the problems were solved and the engagement was established once more. They were married a year later.

"I remember the wedding. . . . They were to be married in Kegalle and five of us were to drive up in Ern's Fiat. Half way between Colombo and Kegalle we recognized a car in the ditch and beside it was the Bishop of Colombo who everyone knew was a terrible driver. He was supposed to marry them so we had to give him a lift.

"First of all his luggage had to be put in carefully because his vestments couldn't be crushed. Then his mitre and sceptre and those special shoes and whatnot. And as we were so crowded and a bishop couldn't sit on anyone's lap — and as no one could really sit on a bishop's lap, we had to let *him* drive the Fiat. We were all so squashed and terrified for the rest of the trip!"

HONEYMOON

The Nuwara Eliya Tennis Championships had ended and there were monsoons in Colombo. The headlines in the local papers said, "Lindbergh's Baby Found — A Corpse!" Fred Astaire's sister, Adele, got married and the 13th President of the French Republic was shot to death by a Russian. The lepers of Colombo went on a hunger strike, a bottle of beer cost one rupee, and there were upsetting rumours that ladies were going to play at Wimbledon in shorts.

In America, women were still trying to steal the body of Valentino from his grave, and a woman from Kansas divorced her husband because he would not let her live near the Valentino mausoleum. The furious impresario, C. B. Cochran, claimed "the ideal modern girl — the Venus of today — should be neither thin nor plump, but should have the lines of a greyhound." It was rumoured that pythons were decreasing in Africa.

Charlie Chaplin was in Ceylon. He avoided all publicity and was only to be seen photographing and studying Kandyan dance. The films at the local cinemas in Colombo were "Love Birds," "Caught Cheating," and "Forbidden Love." There was fighting in Manchuria.

HISTORICAL
RELATIONS

The early twenties had been a busy and expensive time for my grandparents. They spent most of the year in Colombo and during the hot months of April and May moved to Nuwara Eliya. In various family journals there are references made to the time spent "up-country" away from the lowland heat. Cars would leave Colombo and perform the tiring five-hour journey, the radiators steaming as they wound their way up into the mountains. Books and sweaters and golf clubs and rifles were packed into trunks, children were taken out of school, dogs were bathed and made ready for the drive.

Nuwara Eliya was a different world. One did not sweat there and only those who had asthma tried to avoid these vacations. At an elevation of 6000 feet the families could look forward to constant parties, horse racing, the All Ceylon Tennis Tournament, and serious golf. Although the best Sinhalese tennis players competed up-country, they would move back to Colombo if they had to play champions from other nations — as the excessive heat could be guaranteed to destroy the visitors. And so, while monsoon and heat moved into deserted Colombo homes, it was to Nuwara Eliya that my grandparents and their circle of friends would go. They danced in large living rooms to the music of a Bijou-Moutrie piano while the log fires crackled in every room, or on quiet evenings read books on the moonlit porch, slicing open the pages as they progressed through a novel.

The gardens were full of cypress, rhododendrons, fox-gloves, arum-lilies and sweet pea; and people like the van Langenbergs, the Vernon Dickmans, the Henry de Mels and the Philip Ondaatjes were there. There were casual tragedies. Lucas Cantley's wife Jessica almost died after being shot by an unknown assailant while playing croquet with my grandfather. They found 113 pellets in her. "And poor Wilfred Batholomeusz who had large teeth was killed while out hunting when one of his companions mistook him for a wild boar." Most of the men belonged to the CLI reserves and usually borrowed guns when going on vacation.

It was in Nuwara Eliya that Dick de Vos danced with his wife Etta, who fell flat on the floor; she had not danced for years. He picked her up, deposited her on a cane chair, came over to Rex Daniels and said, "Now you know why I gave up dancing and took to drink." Each morning the men departed for the club to play a game of billiards. They would arrive around eleven in buggy carts pulled by bulls and play until the afternoon rest hours while the punkah, the large cloth fan, floated and waved above them and the twenty or so bulls snorted in a circle around the clubhouse. Major Robinson, who ran the prison, would officiate at the tournaments.

During the month of May the circus came to Nuwara Eliya.

Once, when the circus lights failed, Major Robinson drove the fire engine into the tent and focussed the headlights on the trapeze artist, who had no intention of continuing and sat there straddling his trapeze. At one of these touring circuses my Aunt Christie (then only twenty-five) stood up and volunteered to have an apple shot off her head by "a total stranger in the circus profession." That night T. W. Roberts was bitten in the leg by a dog while he danced with her. Later the dog was discovered to be rabid, but as T. W. had left for England nobody bothered to tell him. Most assume he survived. They were all there. Piggford of the police, Paynter the planter, the Finnellis who were Baptist missionaries — "she being an artist and a very good tap dancer."

This was Nuwara Eliya in the twenties and thirties. Everyone was vaguely related and had Sinhalese, Tamil, Dutch, British and Burgher blood in them going back many generations. There was a large social gap between this circle and the Europeans and English who were never part of the Ceylonese community. The English were seen as transients, snobs and racists, and were quite separate from those who had intermarried and who lived here permanently. My father always claimed to be a Ceylon Tamil, though that was probably more valid about three centuries earlier. Emil Daniels summed up the situation for most of them when he was asked by one of the British governors what his nationality was — "God alone knows, your excellency."

The era of grandparents. Philip Ondaatje was supposed to have the greatest collection of wine glasses in the Orient; my other grandfather, Willy Gratiaen, dreamt of snakes. Both my grandmothers lived cautiously, at least until their husbands died. Then they blossomed, especially Lalla who managed to persuade all those she met into chaos. It was Lalla who told us that the twenties were "so whimsical, so busy — that we were always tired."

THE WAR BETWEEN
MEN AND WOMEN

Years later, when Lalla was almost a grandmother, she was standing in the rain at the Pettah market on her way to a party. Money was not so easily available and she did not own a car. When the bus arrived she herded herself in with the rest and, after ten minutes of standing in the aisle, found a seat where three could sit side by side. Eventually the man next to her put his arm behind her shoulder to give them all more room.

Gradually she began to notice the shocked faces of the passengers facing her across the aisle. At first they looked disapprovingly and soon began whispering to each other. Lalla looked at the man next to her who had a smug smile on his face. He seemed to be enjoying himself. Then she looked down and saw that his hand had come over her left shoulder and was squeezing her breast. She smiled to herself.

She had not felt a thing. Her left breast had been removed five years earlier and he was ardently fondling the sponge beneath her gown.

FLAMING YOUTH

Francis Fonseka had the most extreme case of alcoholism in my father's generation and, always the quickest, was the first to drink himself into the grave. He was my father's and Noel's closest friend and the best man at several weddings he tried to spoil. Unambitious, and generous, he lost all his teeth young — something he could never remember doing. When he got into a fight he would remove his false teeth and put them in his back pocket. He was in love for a while with Lorna Piachaud and started fights all over her wedding reception. He even attacked his own wife and then, overcome with guilt, decided to drown himself in a section of the Kandy Lake that was only twelve inches deep. While he crawled around on his hands and knees, H —— consoled Francis' wife as well as he could "and took as much as he could get." If Francis was the extreme alcoholic, H —— was the great rake, his tumescent heart notorious all over Colombo.

Francis and his friends discovered that the cheapest drinks could be found on ships, where alcohol was duty free. Pretending to visit departing relatives, they would board vessels in the harbour and stumble off gangplanks in the early hours of the morning. They were usually ordered out of the lounge when Noel, unable to play a single tune, started thrashing out one of his spontaneous concerts on the piano. Once, when asked to prove who they knew on board, my father opened the first cabin door and claimed a sleeping man as his friend. My father was wearing a tie from his "Cambridge" days and the sleeper, noticing this, groggily vouched for him. They coaxed the sleeper to the bar and my father managed to remember all the Cambridge names, recalling even the exploits of the notorious Sharron K——, who caused havoc with the population of three colleges.

One night Mervyn came to our house and told Vernon, "We're all going to Gasanawa, get dressed." It was one in the morning. Vernon went off to find his clothes and returned to find Mervyn asleep in his bed. He couldn't be moved. You see he just needed a place to sleep.

Gasanawa was the rubber estate where Francis worked and it became the base for most of their parties. Twenty or thirty people would leap into their cars after a tennis tournament or during a boring evening and if the men were already drunk some of the women drove. They all poured out at Gasanawa where they slept in cabins that Francis had built for just such moments. Whenever he was sober, Francis tried to make the estate a perfect place for parties. He lived on gin, tonic-water, and canned meat. He was in the middle of building a tennis court when his boss ordered him to build a proper road into the estate. This took three years because Francis in his enthusiasm built it three times as wide as the main road in Colombo.

People's memories about Gasanawa, even today, are mythic. "There was a lovely flat rock in front of the bungalow where we danced to imported songs such as 'Moonlight Bay' and 'A Fine Romance.'" "A Fine Romance" was always my mother's favourite song. In her sixties I would come across her in the kitchen half singing, *We should be like a couple of hot tomatoes/but you're as cold as yesterday's mashed potatoes.*

So many songs of that period had to do with legumes, fruit and drink. "Yes, we have no bananas," "I've got a lovely bunch of coconuts," "Mung beans on your collar," "The Java Jive." . . . Dorothy Clementi-Smith would sing the solo verses to "There is a tavern in the town" while the others would drunkenly join in on the chorus. Even the shy Lyn Ludowyck betrayed his studies and came out there once, turning out to be a superb mimic, singing both male and female parts from Italian operas which the others had never heard of — so they all thought at first that he was singing a Sinhalese baila.

But for the most part it was the tango that was perfected on that rock at Gasanawa. Casually dressed couples, coated in a thin film of sweat, swirled under the moon to "Rio Rita" by John Bowles on the gramophone, wound up time and again by the drunk Francis. Francis could only dance the tango solo so that he wouldn't do damage to women's feet, for which he had too much respect. He would put on "I kiss your little hand, Madame" and mime great passion for an invisible partner, kissing the mythical hand, pleading to the stars and jungle around him to console him in an unrequited abstract love. He was a great dancer but with a limited endurance. He usually collapsed at the end of his performance, and a woman would sit beside him bathing his head and face with cool water while the others continued dancing.

The parties lasted until the end of the twenties when Francis lost his job over too splendid a road. He was lost to them all by 1935. He was everyone's immaculate, gentle friend, the most forgiven and best-dressed among them, whispering to someone a few seconds before he died, while holding a fish in his hand, "A man *must* have clothes for every occasion."

The waste of youth. Burned purposeless. They forgave that and understood that before everything else. After Francis died there was nowhere really to go. What seemed to follow was a rash of marriages. There had been good times. "Women fought each other like polecats over certain men."

THE BABYLON
STAKES

"The Wall Street crash had a terrible effect on us. Many
of the horses had to be taken over by the military."

The only occupation that
could hope to avert one from
drink and romance was gambling. In India only the aristocracy
gambled; in Ceylon the bankers and lime-burners and fishmongers
and the leisured class would spend their afternoons, shoulder to
shoulder, betting compulsively. The rulers of the country gen-
uinely believed that betting eliminated strikes; men had to work
in order to gamble.

If it was not horses it was crows. A crippled aunt, who could
not get to the track, began the fashion of betting on which crow
would leave a wall first. This proved so popular that the government considered putting a bounty on crows. In any case, soon
after the time Gertie Garvin trained a pet crow, bird-gambling
proved to be untrustworthy. But the real stars were involved
with racing: horses such as "Mordenis," jockeys like "Fordyce," the
trainer "Captain Fenwick." There were racetracks all over the island.

If you sat in the grandstand all bets were five rupees. Then there was the two-rupee enclosure and finally, in the middle of the track, the "gandhi enclosure" where the poorest stood. "From the grandstand you could watch them leaving like ants a good hour before the last race, having lost all their money."

The most dangerous track profession was starter of the race, and one of the few who survived was Clarence de Fonseka, who was famous for knowing every horse in the country by sight. As starter, he positioned himself at the far end of the track. And to forestall threats of death from the crowd in the gandhi enclosure, Clarence kept his fastest horse near him at all times. If a popular horse lost, the mob would race across the field to the starting post to tear him apart. Clarence would then leap onto his horse and gallop down the track in solitary splendour.

Racing concerned everyone. During the whole month of August my mother would close down her dancing school and go to the races. So would my grandmother, Lalla. Her figure at the races is ingrained in several people's memories: a large hat at a rakish angle that she wore with no consideration for anyone behind her, one hand on her hip, one hand on her hat, and a blue jacaranda blossom pinned to the shoulder of her dusty black dress, looking off into the drama of the one-hundred-yard stretch with the intensity of one preparing for the coming of the Magi. When the races were over, groups would depart for dinner, dance till early morning, go swimming and have a breakfast at the Mount Lavinia Hotel. Then to bed till noon when it was time for the races once more. The culmination of the season was the Governor's Cup stakes. Even during the war the August races were not to be postponed. Ceylon could have been invaded during the late afternoon as most of the Light Infantry was at the race track during these hours.

Many of my relatives owned a horse or two, which languished in comfort for much of the year and got trotted out for the August race meet. My grandmother's horse, "Dickman Delight," refused to step out of the stable if it was at all muddy. She would bet vast sums on her horse knowing that one day he would surprise everyone and win. The day this eventually happened, my grandmother was up north. She received a telegram in the early morning which read: "Rain over Colombo" so she put her money on another horse. Dickman Delight galloped to victory on dry turf. Japanese planes had attacked Galle Face Green in Colombo and the telegram should have read: "Raid over Colombo." Dickman Delight never won again.

Most people tried to own a horse, some even pooled their money, each "owning a leg." The desire was not so much to have horse-sense but to be involved with the ceremonial trappings. Percy Lewis de Soysa, for instance, took great care selecting his colours, which were gold and green. In his youth, while successfully entertaining a woman at a Cambridge restaurant, he had ordered a bottle of champagne and at the end of the evening whispered to her that when he eventually owned a horse his racing colours would be taken from the label of the bottle. "Searchlight Gomez" chose his colours, pink and black, after a certain lady's underwear and was proud of it.

There were races all year long. The Monsoon Meet in May, the Hakgalle Stakes in February, the Nuwara Eliya Cup in August. Some of the horses had become so inbred that jockeys could no longer insure themselves. The Babylon Stakes was banned after one horse, "Forced Potato," managed to bite a jockey and then leapt the fence to attack as many as it could in the jeering gandhi enclosure. But the jockeys had their perks. Gambling was so crucial to the economy of certain households that semi-respectable women slept with jockeys to get closer to "the horse's mouth."

If the crowd or the horses did not cause trouble, *The Search-light*, a magazine published by the notorious Mr Gomez, did. "One of those scurrilous things," it attacked starters and trainers and owners and provided gossip to be carefully read between races. Nobody wished to appear in it and everyone bought it. It sold for five cents but remained solvent, as the worst material could be toned down only with bribes to the editor. "Searchlight Gomez," went to jail once, and that for too good a joke. Every January issue featured the upcoming events for the year. One year he listed, under October 3rd, Hayley and Kenny's Annual Fire. This blatant but accurate reference to the way fire insurance was used to compensate for sagging trade was not appreciated and he was sued.

The Gasanawa group tried to take in all the races. In December they drove down to the Galle Gymkhana, stopping on the way to order oysters and have a swim at Ambalangoda. "Sissy," Francis' sister, "was always drowning herself because she was an exhibitionist." The men wore tweed, the women wore their best crinolines. After the races they would return to Ambalangoda, pick up the oysters "which we swallowed with wine if we lost or champagne if we won." Couples then paired off casually or with great complexity and danced in a half-hearted manner to the portable gramophone beside the cars. Ambalangoda was the centre for devil dances and exorcism rites, but this charmed group was part of another lost world. The men leaned their chins against the serene necks of the women, danced a waltz or two, slid oysters into their partner's mouths. The waves on the beach collected champagne corks. Men who had lost fortunes laughed frantically into the night. A woman from the village who was encountered carrying a basket of pineapples was persuaded to trade that for a watch removed from a wrist. Deeper inland at midnight, the devil dances began, drums portioned the night. Trucks carrying horses to the next meet glared their headlights as they passed the group by the side of the road. The horses, drummers, everyone else, seemed to have a purpose. The devil dances cured sickness, catarrh, deafness, aloneness. Here the gramophone accompanied a seduction or an arousal, it spoke of meadows and "little Spanish towns" or "a small hotel," a "blue room."

A hand cupped the heel of a woman who wished to climb a tree to see the stars more clearly. The men laughed into their tumblers. They all went swimming again with just the modesty of the night. An arm touched a face. A foot touched a stomach. They could have almost drowned or fallen in love and their lives would have been totally changed during any one of those evenings.

Then, everyone very drunk, the convoy of cars would race back to Gasanawa in the moonlight crashing into frangipani, almond trees, or slipping off the road to sink slowly up to the door handles in a paddy field.

TROPICAL GOSSIP

"Darling, come here quickly. There's trouble behind the tennis court. I think Frieda's fainted. Look — Craig is pulling her up."

"No, darling, leave them alone."

It seems that most of my relatives at some time were attracted to somebody they shouldn't have been. Love affairs rainbowed over marriages and lasted forever — so it often seemed that marriage was the greater infidelity. From the twenties until the war nobody really had to grow up. They remained wild and spoiled. It was only during the second half of my parents' generation that they suddenly turned to the real world. Years later, for instance, my uncle Noel would return to Ceylon as a Q.C. to argue for the lives of friends from his youth who had tried to overthrow the government.

But earlier, during their flaming youth, this energy formed complex relationships, though I still cannot break the code of how "interested in" or "attracted" they were to each other. Truth disappears with history and gossip tells us in the end nothing of personal relationships. There are stories of elopements, unrequited love, family feuds, and exhausting vendettas, which everyone was drawn into, had to be involved with. But nothing is said of the closeness between two people: how they grew in the shade of each other's presence. No one speaks of that exchange of gift and character — the way a person took on and recognized in himself the smile of a lover. Individuals are seen only in the context of these swirling social tides. It was almost impossible for a couple to do anything without rumour leaving their shoulders like a flock of messenger pigeons.

Where is the intimate and truthful in all this? Teenager and Uncle. Husband and lover. A lost father in his solace. And why do I want to know of this privacy? After the cups of tea, coffee, public conversations . . . I want to sit down with someone and talk with utter directness, want to talk to all the lost history like that deserving lover.

My paternal grandfather —
Philip — was a strict, aloof
man. Most people preferred his brother Aelian who was good-
natured and helpful to everyone. Both were lawyers but my grandfather went on to make huge sums of money in land deals and
retired as he said he would at the age of forty. He built the family
home, "Rock Hill," on a prime spot of land right in the centre of
the town of Kegalle.

"Your great uncle Aelian was a very generous man," says Stanley
Suraweera. "I wanted to learn Latin and he offered to tutor me
from four until five every morning. I'd go to his house by cart
every day and he would be up, waiting for me." In later years
Aelian was to have several heart attacks. In one hospital he was
given so much morphine that he became addicted to it.

My grandfather lived at Rock Hill for most of his life and
ignored everybody in Kegalle social circles. He was immensely

wealthy. Most people considered him a snob, but with his family he was a very loving man. The whole family kissed each other goodnight and good morning, a constant tradition in the house — no matter what chaos my father was causing at the time. Family arguments were buried before bedtime and buried once more first thing in the morning.

So here was "Bampa," as we called him, determined to be a good father and patriarch, spreading a protective wing over his more popular brother Aelian, and living in his empire — acres of choice land in the heart of Kegalle. He was dark and his wife was very white, and a rival for my grandmother's hand remarked that he hoped the children would be striped. The whole family lived in terror of him. Even his strong-willed wife could not blossom till after his death. Like some other Ondaatjes, Bampa had a weakness for pretending to be "English" and, in his starched collars and grey suits, was determined in his customs. My brother, who was only four years old then, still remembers painfully strict meals at Rock Hill with Bampa grinding his teeth at one end of the table — as if his carefully built ceremonies were being evaded by a weak-willed family. It was only in the afternoons when, dressed in sarong and vest, he went out for walks over his property (part of a mysterious treatment for diabetes), that he seemed to become a real part of the landscape around him.

Every two years he would visit England, buy crystal, and learn the latest dances. He was a perfect dancer. Numerous aunts remember him inviting them out in London and taking great pleasure in performing the most recent dance steps with a natural ease. Back home there was enough to worry about. There was Aelian, who was continually giving his money away to ecclesiastical causes, the cousin who was mauled to death by his underfed racehorse, and four star-crossed sisters who were secret drinkers.

Most Ondaatjes liked liquor, sometimes to excess. Most of them were hot tempered — though they blamed diabetes for this whenever possible. And most were genetically attracted to a family called Prins and had to be talked out of marriage — for the Prins brought bad luck wherever they went.

My grandfather died before the war and his funeral was spoken about with outrage and envy for months afterwards. He thought he had organized it well. All the women wore long black dresses and imported champagne was drunk surreptitiously from teacups. But his hope of departing with decorum collapsed before he was put into the ground. His four sisters and my recently liberated grandmother got into a loud argument over whether to pay the men two or three rupees to carry the coffin up the steep slopes to the cemetery. Awkward mourners who had come from Colombo waited as silent as my supine grandfather while the argument blazed from room to room and down the halls of Rock Hill. My grandmother peeled off her long black gloves in fury and refused to proceed with the ceremony, then slid them on with the aid of a daughter when it seemed the body would never leave the house. My father, who was overseeing the cooling of the champagne, was nowhere in sight. My mother and Uncle Aelian retired in a fit of giggles to the garden under the mangosteen tree. All this occurred on the afternoon of September 12, 1938. Aelian died of his liver problems in April of 1942.

*   *   *

For the next decade Rock Hill was seldom used by my family and my father was not to return to it for some years. By that time my parents were divorced and my father had lost various jobs. Bampa had willed the land to his grandchildren but my father, whenever he needed to, would sell or give away sections of land so that houses were gradually built up along the perimeter of the estate. My father returned alone to Kegalle in the late forties and took up farming. He lived quite simply at that time, separate from the earlier circle of friends, and my sister Gillian and I spent most of our holidays with him. By 1950 he had married again and was living with his wife and his two children from his second marriage, Jennifer and Susan.

He ended up, in those later years, concentrating on chickens. His dipsomania would recur every two months or so. Between bouts he would not touch a drink. Then he would be offered one, take it, and would not or could not stop drinking for three or four days. During that time he could do *nothing* but drink. Humorous and gentle when sober, he changed utterly and would do anything to get alcohol. He couldn't eat, had to have a bottle on him at all times. If his new wife Maureen had hidden a bottle, he would bring out his rifle and threaten to kill her. He knew, even when sober, that he would need to drink again, and so buried bottles all around the estate. In the heart of his drunkenness he would remember where the bottles were. He would go into the fowl run, dig under chicken straw, and pull out a half bottle. The cement niches on the side of the house held so many bottles that from the side the building resembled a wine cellar.

He talked to no one on those days, although he recognized friends, was aware of everything that was going on. He had to be at the peak of his intelligence in order to remember exactly where the bottles were so he could outwit his wife and family. Nobody could stop him. If Maureen managed to destroy the bottles of gin he had hidden he would drink methylated spirits. He drank until he collapsed and passed out. Then he would waken and drink again. Still no food. Sleep. Get up and have one more shot and then he was finished. He would not drink again for about two months, not until the next bout.

The day my father died, Stanley Suraweera, now a Proctor at Kegalle, was in Court when a messenger brought him the note: *Mervyn has dropped dead. What shall I do? Maureen.*

*   *   *

We had spent three days in Upcot in beautiful tea country with my half-sister Susan. On the way back to Colombo we drove through the Kadugannawa Pass and stopped at Kegalle. The old wooden bridge that only my father drove over without fear ("God loves a drunk" he would say to anyone who sat by him white with terror) had been replaced with a concrete one.

What to us had been a lovely spacious house was now small and dark, fading into the landscape. A Sinhalese family occupied Rock Hill. Only the mangosteen tree, which I practically lived in as a child during its season of fruit, was full and strong. At the back, the kitul tree still leaned against the kitchen — tall, with tiny yellow berries which the polecat used to love. Once a week it would climb up and spend the morning eating the berries and come down drunk, would stagger over the lawn pulling up flowers or come into the house to up-end drawers of cutlery and serviettes. Me and my polecat, my father said after one occasion when their drunks coincided, my father lapsing into his songs — baila or heartbreaking Rodgers and Hart or his own version of "My Bonnie Lies over the Ocean" —

My whiskey comes over the ocean
My brandy comes over the sea
But my beer comes from F.X. Pereira

So F.X. Pereira for me.

F.X. . . . F.X. . . .

F.X. Pereira for me, for me. . . .

He emerged out of his bedroom to damn whoever it was that was playing the piano — to find the house empty — Maureen and the kids having left, and the polecat walking up and down over the keys breaking the silence of the house, oblivious to his human audience; and my father wishing to celebrate this companionship, discovering all the bottles gone, unable to find anything, finally walking up to the kerosene lamp hanging in the centre of the room at head level, and draining *that* liquid into his mouth. He and his polecat.

Gillian remembered some of the places where he hid bottles. *Here* she said, *and here*. Her family and my family walked around the house, through the depressed garden of guava trees, plantains, old forgotten flowerbeds. Whatever "empire" my grandfather had fought for had to all purposes disappeared.

DON'T TALK TO ME
ABOUT MATISSE

TABULA ASIAE

On my brother's wall in Toronto are the false maps. Old portraits of Ceylon. The result of sightings, glances from trading vessels, the theories of sextant. The shapes differ so much they seem to be translations — by Ptolemy, Mercator, François Valentyn, Mortier, and Heydt — growing from mythic shapes into eventual accuracy. Amoeba, then stout rectangle, and then the island as we know it now, a pendant off the ear of India. Around it, a blue-combed ocean busy with dolphin and sea-horse, cherub and compass. Ceylon floats on the Indian Ocean and holds its naive mountains, drawings of cassowary and boar who leap without perspective across imagined "desertum" and plain.

At the edge of the maps the scrolled mantling depicts ferocious slipper-footed elephants, a white queen offering a necklace to natives who carry tusks and a conch, a Moorish king who stands amidst the power of books and armour. On the south-west corner of some charts are satyrs, hoof deep in foam, listening to the sound of the island, their tails writhing in the waves.

The maps reveal rumours of topography, the routes for invasion and trade, and the dark mad mind of travellers' tales appears throughout Arab and Chinese and medieval records. The island seduced all of Europe. The Portuguese. The Dutch. The English. And so its name changed, as well as its shape — Serendip, Ratnapida ("island of gems"), Taprobane, Zeloan, Zeilan, Seyllan, Ceilon, and Ceylon — the wife of many marriages, courted by invaders who stepped ashore and claimed everything with the power of their sword or bible or language.

This pendant, once its shape stood still, became a mirror. It pretended to reflect each European power till newer ships arrived and spilled their nationalities, some of whom stayed and intermarried — my own ancestor arriving in 1600, a doctor who cured the residing governor's daughter with a strange herb and was rewarded with land, a foreign wife, and a new name which was a Dutch spelling of his own. Ondaatje. A parody of the ruling language. And when his Dutch wife died, marrying a Sinhalese woman, having nine children, and remaining. Here. At the centre of the rumour. At this point on the map.

ST. THOMAS' CHURCH

In Colombo a church faces west into the sea. We drive along Reclamation Street through markets and boutiques. The church ahead of us is painted a pale dirty blue. Below us, an oil-tanker dwarfs the harbour and the shops. We get out, followed by the children. A path about twelve feet wide bordered by plantain trees. The gothic doors give a sense, as all church doors do, of being wheeled open. Inside are wooden pews and their geometrical shadows and stone floors that whisper against the children's bare feet. We spread out.

After all these generations the coming darkness makes it necessary to move fast in order to read the brass plaques on the walls. The first ones are too recent, 19th century. Then, by the communion rail, I see it — cut across the stone floor. To kneel on the floors of a church built in 1650 and see your name chiseled in large letters so that it stretches from your fingertips to your elbow in some strange way removes vanity, eliminates the personal. It makes your own story a lyric. So the sound which came immediately out of my mouth as I half-gasped and called my sister spoke all that excitement of smallness, of being overpowered by stone.

What saved me was the lack of clarity. The slab was five feet long, three feet wide, a good portion of it had worn away. We remained on our knees in that fading light, asked the children to move their shadows, and peered sideways to try to catch the faint ridge of letters worn away by the traffic of feet. The light leaned into the chiseled area like frail sand. To the right of that slab was another; we had been standing on it totally unaware, as if in someone's rifle sight. Gillian wrote on a brown envelope as I read

Sacred to the memory of Natalia Asarrapa — wife of Philip Jurgen Ondaatje. Born 1797, married 1812, died 1822, age 25 years.

She was fifteen! That can't be right. Must be. Fifteen when she married and twenty-five when she died. Perhaps that was the first wife — before he married Jacoba de Melho? Probably another branch of the family.

We carry six ledgers out of the church into the last of the sunlight and sit on the vicarage steps to begin reading. Lifting the ancient pages and turning them over like old, skeletal leaves. The black script must have turned brown over a hundred years ago. The thick pages foxed and showing the destruction caused by silverfish, scars among the immaculate recordings of local history and formal signatures. We had not expected to find more than one Ondaatje here but the stones and pages are full of them. We had been looking for the Reverend Jurgen Ondaatje — a translator and eventual chaplain in Colombo from 1835 until 1847. It seems, however, as if every Ondaatje for miles around flocked here to be baptised and married. When Jurgen died his son Simon took his place and was the last Tamil Colonial Chaplain of Ceylon.

Simon was the oldest of four brothers. Every Sunday morning they came to this church in carriages with their wives and children and after the service retired to the vicarage for drinks and lunch. Just before the meal, talk would erupt into a violent argument and each brother would demand to have his carriage brought round, climb into it with his hungry family and ride off to his own home, each in a different direction.

For years they tried but were never able to have a meal together. Each of them was prominent in his own field and was obviously too didactic and temperamental to agree with his brothers on any subject of discussion. There was nothing one could speak about that would not infringe on another's area of interest. If the subject was something as innocent as flowers, then Dr. William Charles Ondaatje, who was the Ceylonese Director of the Botanical Gardens, would throw scorn on any opinion and put the others in their place. He had introduced the olive to Ceylon. Finance or military talk was Matthew Ondaatje's area, and law or scholarship exercised Philip de Melho Jurgen's acid tongue. The only one who had full freedom was the Reverend Simon who said whatever he felt like during the sermon, knowing his brothers could not interrupt him. No doubt he caught hell as soon as he entered the vicarage next door for what he hoped would be a peaceful lunch. Whenever a funeral or baptism occurred, however, all the brothers would be there. The church records show Simon's name witnessing them all in a signature very like my father's.

We stand outside the church in twilight. The building has stood here for over three hundred years, in the palm of monsoons, through seasonal droughts and invasions from other countries. Its grounds were once beautiful. Lights begin to come on slowly below us in the harbour. As we are about to get into the Volks, my niece points to a grave and I start walking through the brush in my sandals. "Watch out for snakes!" God. I make a quick leap backwards and get into the car. Night falls quickly during the five minute drive back to the house. Sit down in my room and transcribe names and dates from the various envelopes into a notebook. When I finish there will be that eerie moment when I wash my hands and see very clearly the deep grey colour of old paper dust going down the drain.

MONSOON
NOTEBOOK (i)

To jungles and gravestones.
. . . Reading torn 100-year-old newspaper clippings that come apart in your hands like wet sand, information tough as plastic dolls. Watched leopards sip slowly, watched the crow sitting restless on his branch peering about with his beak open. Have seen the outline of a large fish caught and thrown in the curl of a wave, been where nobody wears socks, where you wash your feet before you go to bed, where I watch my sister who alternatively reminds me of my father, mother and brother. Driven through rainstorms that flood the streets for an hour and suddenly evaporate, where sweat falls in the path of this ballpoint, where the jak fruit rolls across your feet in the back of the jeep, where there are eighteen ways of describing the smell of a durian, where bullocks hold up traffic and steam after the rains.

Have sat down to meals and noticed the fan stir in all the spoons on the dining table. And driven that jeep so often I didn't have time to watch the country slide by thick with event, for everything came directly to me and passed me like snow. The black thick feather of bus exhaust everyone was sentimental against, the man vomiting out of a window, the pig just dead having his hairs burnt off on the Canal Road and old girlfriends from childhood who now towel their kids dry on the other side of the SSC pool, and my watch collecting sea under the glass and gleaming with underwater phosphorus by my bed at night, the inside of both my feet blistering in my first week from the fifteen-cent sandals and the obsessional sarong buying in Colombo, Kandy, Jaffna, Trincomalee, the toddy drink I got subtly smashed on by noon so I slept totally unaware of my dreams. And women and men with naked feet under the dinner table, and after the party the thunderstorm we walked through for five seconds from porch to car, thoroughly soaked and by the time we had driven ten minutes — without headlights which had been stolen that afternoon at the pool — we were dry just from the midnight heat inside the vehicle and the ghosts of steam cruising disorganized off the tarmac roads, and the man sleeping on the street who objected when I woke him each of us talking different languages, me miming a car coming around the corner and hitting him and he, drunk, perversely making me perform this action for him again and again, and I got back into the car fully wet once more and again dry in five miles. And the gecko on the wall waving his tail stiffly his jaws full of dragonfly whose wings symmetrically disappeared into his mouth — darkness filling the almost transparent body, and a yellow enamel-assed spider crossing the bidet and the white rat my daughter claims she saw in the toilet at the Maskeliya tennis club.

I witnessed everything. One morning I would wake and just smell things for the whole day, it was so rich I had to select senses. And still everything moved slowly with the assured fateful speed of a coconut falling on someone's head, like the Jaffna train, like the fan at low speed, like the necessary sleep in the afternoon with dreams blinded by toddy.

TONGUE

In the early afternoon several children and I walk for an hour along the beach — from the foot of the garden at Uswetakeiyawa, past the wrecks, to the Pegasus Reef Hotel. After twenty minutes, with sun burning just the right side of our faces and bodies, climbing up and down the dunes, we are exhausted, feel drunk. One of my children talking about some dream she had before leaving Canada. Spray breaking and blazing white. Mad dog heat. On our left the cool dark of village trees. Crabs veer away from our naked steps. I keep counting the children, keep feeling that one is missing. We look down, away from the sun. So that we all suddenly stumble across the body.

From the back it looks like a crocodile. It is about eight feet long. The snout however is blunt, not pointed, as if a crocodile's nose has been chopped off and the sharp edges worn smooth by tides. For a moment I actually believe this. I don't want the others going too close in case it is not dead. It has a double row of pointed scales on its tail, and the grey body is covered in yellow spots — with black centres so they form yellow rings. He looks fat and bulky. No one from the village about ten yards away seems to have noticed him. I realize it is a kabaragoya. In English a sub-aquatic monitor. He is dangerous and can whip you to death with his tail. This creature must have been washed out to sea by a river and then drifted back onto the beach.

Kabaragoyas and thalagoyas are common in Ceylon and are seldom found anywhere else in the world. The kabaragoya is large, the size of an average crocodile, and the thalagoya smaller — a cross between an iguana and a giant lizard. Sir John Maundeville, one of the first travellers to write of Ceylon, speaks of their "schorte thyes and grete Nayles." And Robert Knox says of the kabaragoya that "he hath a blew forked tongue like a string, which he puts forth and hisseth and gapeth." The kabaragoya is in fact a useful scavenger and is now protected by law as it preys on fresh water crabs that undermine and ruin the bunds of paddy fields. The only thing that will scare it is a wild boar.

The thalagoya, on the other hand, will eat snails, beetles, centipedes, toads, skinks, eggs and young birds, and is not averse to garbage. It is also a great climber, and can leap forty feet from a tree to the ground, breaking its fall by landing obliquely with its chest, belly and tail. In Kegalle the thalagoyas would climb trees and leap onto the roof or into the house.

The thalagoya has a rasping tongue that "catches" and hooks objects. There is a myth that if a child is given thalagoya tongue to eat he will become brilliantly articulate, will always speak beautifully, and in his speech be able to "catch" and collect wonderful, humorous information.

There is a way to eat the tongue. The thalagoya is killed by placing it on the ground, doubling its head under the throat, and striking the nape with a clenched fist. The tongue should be sliced off and eaten as soon as possible after the animal dies. You take a plantain or banana, remove the skin and cut it lengthwise in half, place the grey tongue between two pieces of banana making a sandwich, and then swallow the thing without chewing, letting it slide down the throat whole. Many years later this will result in verbal brilliance, though sometimes this will be combined with bad behaviour (the burning of furniture, etc.). I am not sure what other side effects there are apart from possible death.

My Uncle Noel was given a thalagoya tongue. He spat half of it out, got very sick and nearly died. His mother, Lalla, who had a habit of throwing herself dangerously into such local practices, had insisted he eat it. In any case her son did become a brilliant lawyer and a great story teller, from eating just *part* of the tongue. My father, who was well aware of the legend, suggested we eat some when we were in the Ambalantota resthouse. One had just been killed there, having fallen through the roof. All the children hid screaming in the bathroom until it was time to leave.

The thalagoya has other uses. It has the only flesh that can be kept down by a persistently vomiting patient and is administered to pregnant women for morning sickness. But as children we knew exactly what thalagoyas and kabaragoyas were good for. The kabaragoya laid its eggs in the hollows of trees between the months of January and April. As this coincided with the Royal-Thomian cricket match, we would collect them and throw them into the stands full of Royal students. These were great weapons because they left a terrible itch wherever they splashed on skin. We used the thalagoya to scale walls. We tied a rope around its neck and heaved it over a wall. Its claws could cling to any surface, and we pulled ourselves up the rope after it.

About six months before I was born my mother observed a pair of kabaragoyas "in copula" at Pelmadulla. A reference is made to this sighting in *A Coloured Atlas of Some Vertebrates from Ceylon, Vol. 2*, a National Museums publication. It is my first memory.

SWEET LIKE A CROW

for Hetti Corea, 8 years old

*"The Sinhalese are beyond a doubt one of the least
musical people in the world. It would be quite impossible to have less sense of pitch, line, or rhythm."*

PAUL BOWLES

Your voice sounds like a scorpion being pushed
through a glass tube
like someone has just trod on a peacock
like wind howling in a coconut
like a rusty bible, like someone pulling barbed wire
across a stone courtyard, like a pig drowning,
a vattacka being fried
a bone shaking hands
a frog singing at Carnegie Hall.
Like a crow swimming in milk,
like a nose being hit by a mango
like the crowd at the Royal-Thomian match,
a womb full of twins, a pariah dog
with a magpie in its mouth
like the midnight jet from Casablanca
like Air Pakistan curry,

a typewriter on fire, like a spirit in the gas
which cooks your dinner,
like a hundred pappadans being crunched, like someone
uselessly trying to light 3 *Roses* matches in a dark room,
the clicking sound of a reef when you put your head into the sea,
a dolphin reciting epic poetry to a sleepy audience,
the sound of a fan when someone throws brinjals at it,
like pineapples being sliced in the Pettah market
like betel juice hitting a butterfly in mid-air
like a whole village running naked onto the street
and tearing their sarongs, like an angry family
pushing a jeep out of the mud, like dirt on the needle,
like 8 sharks being carried on the back of a bicycle
like 3 old ladies locked in the lavatory
like the sound I heard when having an afternoon sleep
and someone walked through my room in ankle bracelets.

THE KARAPOTHAS

"This Ceylon part of the journey goes wearily! wearily! Tired out by being constantly disturbed all night — noisy sea, and noisier soda-bottle-popping planters, and the early dawn with crows and cocks.

The brown people of this island seem to me odiously inquisitive and bothery-idiotic. All the while the savages go on grinning and chattering to each other.

. . . The roads are intensely picturesque. Animals, apes, porcupine, hornbill, squirrel, pidgeons, and figurative dirt!"

From the journals of Edward Lear in Ceylon, 1875

"After all, Taormina, Ceylon, Africa, America — as far as *we* go, they are only the negation of what we ourselves stand for and are: and we're rather like Jonahs running away from the place we belong.

. . . Ceylon is an experience — but heavens, not a permanence."

D.H. Lawrence

"All jungles are evil."

Leonard Woolf

*   *   *

I sit in a house on Buller's Road. I am the foreigner. I am the prodigal who hates the foreigner. Looking out on overgrown garden and the two dogs who bark at everything, who fling themselves into the air towards bird and squirrel. Ants crawl onto the desk to taste whatever is placed here. Even my glass, which holds just ice water, has brought out a dozen who wade into the rim of liquid the tumbler leaves, checking it for sugar. We are back within the heat of Colombo, in the hottest month of the year. It is delicious heat. Sweat runs with its own tangible life down a body as if a giant egg has been broken onto our shoulders.

The most comfortable hours are from 4 A.M. until about nine in the morning; the rest of the day heat walks the house as an animal hugging everybody. No one moves too far from the circumference of the fan. Rich Sinhalese families go up-country during April. Most of the events in the erotic literature of Asia, one suspects, must take place in the mountains, for sex is almost impossible in Colombo except in the early morning hours, and very few have been conceived during this month for the last hundred years.

This is the heat that drove Englishmen crazy. D.H. Lawrence was in Ceylon for six weeks in 1922 as a guest of the Brewsters who lived in Kandy. Even though Kandy is several degrees cooler than Colombo, his cantankerous nature rose to the surface like sweat. He found the Sinhalese far too casual and complained about "the papaw-stinking buddhists." On his first day the Brewsters took him for a walk around Kandy Lake. Achsah and Earl Brewster describe how Lawrence pulled out his silver watch and noticed that it had stopped. He went into a rage, heaving and pulling to break the chain, and threw the watch into the lake. The silver time-piece floated down and joined more significant unrecovered treasure buried by Kandyan kings.

Heat disgraces foreigners. Yesterday, on the road from Kandy to Colombo we passed New Year's festivities in every village — grease pole climbing, bicycle races with roadside crowds heaving buckets of water over the cyclists as they passed — everyone joining in the ceremonies during the blazing noon. But my kids, as we drove towards lowland heat, growing belligerent and yelling at each other to shut up, shut up, shut up.

Two miles away from Buller's Road lived another foreigner. Pablo Neruda. For two years during the thirties, he lived in Wellawatte while working for the Chilean Embassy. He had just escaped from Burma and Josie Bliss of "The widower's tango" and in his *Memoirs* writes mostly about his pet mongoose. An aunt of mine remembers his coming to dinner and continually breaking into song, but many of his dark claustrophobic pieces in *Residence on Earth* were written here, poems that saw this landscape governed by a crowded surrealism — full of vegetable oppressiveness.

Ceylon always did have too many foreigners . . . the "Karapothas" as my niece calls them — the beetles with white spots who never grew ancient here, who stepped in and admired the landscape, disliked the "inquisitive natives" and left. They came originally and overpowered the land obsessive for something as delicate as the smell of cinnamon. Becoming wealthy with spices. When ships were still approaching, ten miles out at sea, captains would spill cinnamon onto the deck and invite passengers on board to *smell Ceylon* before the island even came into view.

"From Seyllan to Paradise is forty miles," says a legend, "the sound of the fountains of Paradise is heard there." But when Robert Knox was held captive on the island in the 17th century he remembered his time this way: "Thus was I left Desolate, Sick and in Captivity, having no earthly comforter, none but only He who looks down from Heaven to hear the groaning of the prisoners."

The leap from one imagination to the other can hardly be made; no more than Desdemona could understand truly the Moor's military exploits. We own the country we grow up in, or we are aliens and invaders. Othello's talent was a decorated sleeve she was charmed by. This island was a paradise to be sacked. Every conceivable thing was collected and shipped back to Europe: cardamons, pepper, silk, ginger, sandalwood, mustard oil, palmyra root, tamarind, wild indigo, deers' horns, elephant tusks, hog lard, calamander, coral, seven kinds of cinnamon, pearl and cochineal. *A perfumed sea.*

And if this was paradise, it had a darker side. My ancestor, William Charles Ondaatje, knew of at least fifty-five species of poisons easily available to his countrymen, none of it, it seems,

63

used against the invaders. Varieties of arsenic, juices from the centipede, scorpion, toad and glow-worm, jackal and "mungoose," ground blue peacock stones — these could stun a man into death in minutes. "Croton seeds are used as a means to facilitate theft and other criminal intentions," he wrote in his biological notebooks. In his most lyrical moment, in footnote 28 of his report on the Royal Botanic Gardens, William Charles steps away from the formal paper, out of the latinized garden, and, with the passion of a snail or bird, gifts us his heart.

> Here are majestic palms with their towering stems and graceful foliage, the shoe flower, the eatable passion flower. Here the water lily swims the rivers with expanded leaves — a prince of aquatic plants! The Aga-mula-naeti-wala, *creeper without beginning or end*, twines around trees and hangs in large festoons . . . and curious indeed these are from having neither leaves nor roots. Here is the winged thunbergia, the large snouted justicia, the mustard tree of Scripture with its succulent leaves and infinitesimal berries. The busy acacia with its sweet fragrance perfumes the dreary plains while other sad and un-named flowers sweeten the night with their blossoms which are shed in the dark.

The journals delight in the beauty and the poisons, he invents "paper" out of indigenous vegetables, he tests local medicines and poisons on dogs and rats. "A man at Jaffna committed suicide by eating the *neagala* root. . . . A concoction of the plumbago is given to produce abortion." Casually he lists the possible weapons around him. The karapothas crawled over them and admired their beauty.

The island hid its knowledge. Intricate arts and customs and religious ceremonies moved inland away from the new cities. Only

Robert Knox, held captive by a Kandyan king for twenty years, wrote of the island well, learning its traditions. His memoir, *An Historical Relation*, was used by Defoe as a psychological source for the ever inquisitive Robinson Crusoe. "If you peer into the features of Crusoe you will see something of the man who was not the lonely inhabitant of a desert island but who lived in an alien land among strangers, cut away from his own countrymen . . . and striving hard not only to return but also to employ profitably the single talent that had been given him."

Apart from Knox, and later Leonard Woolf in his novel, *A Village in the Jungle*, very few foreigners truly knew where they were.

* * *

I still believe the most beautiful alphabet was created by the Sinhalese. The insect of ink curves into a shape that is almost sickle, spoon, eyelid. The letters are washed blunt glass which betray no jaggedness. Sanskrit was governed by verticals, but its sharp grid features were not possible in Ceylon. Here the Ola leaves which people wrote on were too brittle. A straight line would cut apart the leaf and so a curling alphabet was derived from its Indian cousin. Moon coconut. The bones of a lover's spine.

When I was five — the only time in my life when my handwriting was meticulous — I sat in the tropical classrooms and learned the letters ᴁ, and ᴓ, repeating them page after page. How to write. The self-portrait of language. ᴕ Lid on a cooking utensil that takes the shape of fire. Years later, looking into a biology textbook, I came across a whole page depicting the small bones in the body and recognized, delighted, the shapes and forms of the first alphabet I ever copied from Kumarodaya's first grade reader.

At St. Thomas' College Boy School I had written "lines" as punishment. A hundred and fifty times. කොපල්ස්ටන් නිවෙසේ වහලයට නැගි පොල්ගෙඩි විසි කොනරමි. I must not throw coconuts off the roof of Copplestone House. බාර්නබස් පියතුමාගේ කාරයේ වයර්වලට සිසිදා මුතු කොනරමි. We must not urinate again on Father Barnabus' tires. A communal protest this time, the first of my socialist tendencies. The idiot phrases moved east across the page as if searching for longitude and story, some meaning or grace that would occur *blazing* after so much writing. For years I thought literature was punishment, simply a parade ground. The only freedom writing brought was as the author of rude expressions on walls and desks.

In the 5th Century B.C. graffiti poems were scratched onto the rock face of Sigiriya — the rock fortress of a despot king. Short verses to the painted women in the frescoes which spoke of love in all its confusions and brokenness. Poems to mythological women who consumed and overcame mundane lives. The phrases saw breasts as perfect swans; eyes were long and clean as horizons. The anonymous poets returned again and again to the same metaphors. Beautiful *false compare*. These were the first folk poems of the country.

When the government rounded up thousands of suspects during the Insurgency of 1971, the Vidyalankara campus of the University of Ceylon was turned into a prison camp. The police weeded out the guilty, trying to break their spirit. When the university opened again the returning students found hundreds of poems written on walls, ceilings, and in hidden corners of the campus. Quatrains and free verse about the struggle, tortures, the unbroken spirit, love of friends who had died for the cause. The students went around for days transcribing them into their notebooks before they were covered with whitewash and lye.

*　　*　　*

I spend hours talking with Ian Goonetileke, who runs the library at Peradeniya, about writers in Ceylon. He shows me a book he put together on the Insurgency. Because of censorship it had to be published in Switzerland. At the back of the book are ten photographs of charcoal drawings done by an insurgent on the walls of one of the houses he hid in. The average age of the insurgents was seventeen and thousands were killed by police and army. While the Kelani and Mahaveli rivers moved to the sea, heavy with bodies, these drawings were destroyed so that the book is now the only record of them. The artist is anonymous. The works seem as great as the Sigiriya frescoes. They too need to be eternal.

He also shows me the poetry of Lakdasa Wikkramasinha, one of his close friends who drowned recently at Mount Lavinia. A powerful and angry poet. Lakdasa was two years ahead of me at St. Thomas' College and though I never knew him we had studied in the same classrooms and with the same teachers.

As I leave his house, Ian returns to the beautiful George Keyt drawings which fill his study and the books he has to publish in other countries in order to keep the facts straight, the legends uncovered. He is a man who knows history is always present, is the last hour of his friend Lakdasa blacking out in the blue sea at Mount Lavinia where the tourists go to sunbathe, is the burned down wall that held those charcoal drawings whose passionate conscience should have been cut into rock. The voices I didn't know. The visions which are anonymous. And secret.

This morning in the house on Buller's Road I read the poetry of Lakdasa Wikkramasinha.

> *Don't talk to me about Matisse . . .*
> *the European style of 1900, the tradition of the studio*
> *where the nude woman reclines forever*
> *on a sheet of blood*
> *Talk to me instead of the culture generally —*
> *how the murderers were sustained*
> *by the beauty robbed of savages: to our remote*
> *villages the painters came, and our white-washed*
> *mud-huts were splattered with gunfire.*

HIGH FLOWERS

The slow moving of her cotton
in the heat.
                Hard shell of foot.
She chops the yellow coconut
the colour of Anuradhapura stone.

The woman my ancestors ignored
sits at the doorway chopping coconut
cleaning rice.

Her husband moves
in the air between trees.
The curved knife at his hip.
In high shadows
of coconut palms
he grasps a path of rope above his head

and another below him with his naked foot.
He drinks the first sweet mouthful
from the cut flower, then drains it
into a narrow-necked pot
and steps out to the next tree.

Above the small roads of Wattala,
Kalutara, the toddy tapper walks
collecting the white liquid for tavern vats.
Down here the light
storms through branches
and boils the street.
Villagers stand in the shadow and drink
the fluid from a coned leaf.
He works fast to reach his quota
before the maniac monsoon.
The shape of knife and pot
do not vary from 18th Century museum prints.

In the village,
a woman shuffles rice
in a cane mat.
Grit and husk separate
are thrown to the sun.

From his darkness among high flowers
to this room contained by mud walls
everything that is important occurs in shadow —
her discreet slow moving his dreams of walking
from tree to tree without ropes.
It is not vanity which allows him this freedom

but skill and habit, the curved knife
his father gave him, it is the coolness up there
— for the ground's heat has not yet risen —
which makes him forget necessity.

Kings. Fortresses. Traffic in open sun.

Within a doorway the woman
turns in the old pleasure of darkness.

In the high trees above her
shadows eliminate
the path he moves along.

TO COLOMBO

Returning from Sigiriya hills
in their high green the grey
animal fortress rock claws of stone
rumours of wild boar

pass

paddy terraces
bullocks brown men
who rise knee deep like the earth
out of the earth

Sunlight Sunlight

stop for the cool *kurumba*
scoop the half formed white
into our mouths

remove

tarpaulin walls of the jeep
to receive lowland air

on a bench behind sunlight
the woman the coconuts the knife

WOMEN LIKE YOU

(the communal poem — Sigiri Graffiti, 5th century)

They do not stir
these ladies of the mountain
do not give us
the twitch of eyelids.

                The king is dead.

They answer no one
take the hard
rock as lover.
Women like you
make men pour out their hearts

                  'Seeing you I want
                  no other life'

'The golden skins have
caught my mind'

who came here
out of the bleached land
climbed this fortress
to adore the rock
and with the solitude of the air
behind them
                carved an alphabet
whose motive was perfect desire

wanting these portraits of women
to speak
and caress.

Hundreds of small verses
by different hands
became one
habit of the unrequited.

Seeing you
I want no other life
and turn around
to the sky
and everywhere below
jungle, waves of heat
secular love

Holding the new flowers
a circle of

first finger and thumb
which is a window

to your breast

pleasure of the skin
earring earring
curl
of the belly
              and then
stone mermaid
stone heart
dry as a flower
on rock
you long eyed women
the golden
drunk swan breasts
lips
the long long eyes

we stand against the sky

I bring you

a flute
from the throat
of a loon

so talk to me
of the used heart

THE CINNAMON
PEELER

If I were a cinnamon peeler
I would ride your bed
and leave the yellow bark dust
on your pillow.

Your breasts and shoulders would reek
you could never walk through markets
without the profession of my fingers
floating over you. The blind would
stumble certain of whom they approached
though you might bathe
under rain gutters, monsoon.

Here on the upper thigh
at this smooth pasture
neighbour to your hair

or the crease
that cuts your back. This ankle.
You will be known among strangers
as the cinnamon peeler's wife.

I could hardly glance at you
before marriage
never touch you
— your keen nosed mother, your rough brothers.
I buried my hands
in saffron, disguised them
over smoking tar,
helped the honey gatherers . . .

                    *

When we swam once
I touched you in water
and our bodies remained free,
you could hold me and be blind of smell.
You climbed the bank and said

                    this is how you touch other women
the grass cutter's wife, the lime burner's daughter.
And you searched your arms
for the missing perfume
                    and knew

                    what good is it
to be the lime burner's daughter
left with no trace

as if not spoken to in the act of love
as if wounded without the pleasure of a scar.

You touched
your belly to my hands
in the dry air and said
I am the cinnamon
peeler's wife. Smell me.

KEGALLE (ii)

The family home of Rock Hill was littered with snakes, especially cobras. The immediate garden was not so dangerous, but one step further and you would see several. The chickens that my father kept in later years were an even greater magnet. The snakes came for the eggs. The only deterrent my father discovered was ping-pong balls. He had crates of ping-pong balls shipped to Rock Hill and distributed them among the eggs. The snake would swallow the ball whole and be unable to digest it. There are several paragraphs on this method of snake control in a pamphlet he wrote on poultry farming.

The snakes also had the habit of coming into the house and at least once a month there would be shrieks, the family would run around, the shotgun would be pulled out, and the snake would be blasted to pieces. Certain sections of the walls and floors showed the scars of shot. My stepmother found one coiled asleep on her desk and was unable to approach the drawer to get the key to open the gun case. At another time one lay sleeping on the large radio to draw its warmth and, as nobody wanted to destroy the one source of music in the house, this one was watched carefully but left alone.

Most times though there would be running footsteps, yells of fear and excitement, everybody trying to quiet everybody else, and my father or stepmother would blast away not caring what was in the background, a wall, good ebony, a sofa, or a decanter. They killed at least thirty snakes between them.

After my father died, a grey cobra came into the house. My stepmother loaded the gun and fired at point blank range. The gun jammed. She stepped back and reloaded but by then the snake had slid out into the garden. For the next month this snake would often come into the house and each time the gun would misfire or jam, or my stepmother would miss at absurdly short range. The snake attacked no one and had a tendency to follow my younger sister Susan around. Other snakes entering the house were killed by the shotgun, lifted with a long stick and flicked into the bushes, but the old grey cobra led a charmed life. Finally one of the old workers at Rock Hill told my stepmother what had become obvious, that it was my father who had come to protect his family. And in fact, whether it was because the chicken farm closed down or because of my father's presence in the form of a snake, very few other snakes came into the house again.

*   *   *

The last incident at Rock Hill took place in 1971, a year before the farm was sold. 1971 was the year of the Insurgence. The rebels against the government consisted of thousands from every walk of life — but essentially the young. The age of an insurgent ranged from fifteen to twenty. They were a strange mixture of innocence and determination and anarchy, making home-made bombs with nails and scraps of metal and at the same time delighted and proud of their uniforms of blue trousers with a stripe down the side, and tennis shoes. Some had never worn tennis shoes before. My cousin Rhunie was staying at the Ambepussa resthouse with the Chitrasena dance troupe when fifty insurgents marched up the road in formation chanting "we are hungry we are hungry," ransacked the place for food, but did not touch any one there because they were all fans of the dance company.

The insurgents were remarkably well organized and general belief is that they would have taken over the country if one group hadn't mixed up the dates and attacked the police station in Wellawaya a day too soon. The following day every police station and every army barrack and every radio station was to be hit simultaneously. Some gangs hid out in the jungle reserves at Wilpattu and Yala where they survived by shooting and eating the wildlife. A week before the uprising they had broken into local government offices, gone through the files and found the location of every registered weapon in the country. The day after the revolt broke out, a gang of twenty marched from house to house in Kegalle collecting weapons and finally came up the hill to Rock Hill.

They had ransacked several houses already, stripping them of everything — food, utensils, radios and clothing, but this group of 17-year-olds was extremely courteous to my stepmother and her children. My father had apparently donated several acres of Rock Hill towards a playground several years earlier and many of these insurgents had known him well.

They asked for whatever weapons the house had and my step-mother handed over the notorious shotgun. They checked their files and saw a rifle was also listed. It turned out to be an air rifle, wrongly categorized. I had used it often as a ten-year-old, ankle deep in paddy fields, shooting at birds, and if there were no birds, at the fruit of trees. While all this official business was going on around the front porch, the rest of the insurgents had put down their huge collection of weapons, collected from all over Kegalle, and persuaded my younger sister Susan to provide a bat and a tennis ball. Asking her to join them, they proceeded to play a game of cricket on the front lawn. They played for most of the afternoon.

ECLIPSE
PLUMAGE

LUNCH
CONVERSATION

Wait a minute, wait a minute! When did all this happen, I'm trying to get it straight . . .

Your mother was nine, Hilden was there, and your grandmother Lalla and David Grenier and his wife Dickie.

How old was Hilden?

Oh, in his early twenties.

But Hilden was having dinner with my mother and you.

Yes, says Barbara. And Trevor de Saram. And Hilden and your mother and I were quite drunk. It was a wedding lunch, Babette's

I think, I can't remember all those weddings. I know Hilden was moving with a rotten crowd of drinkers then so he was drunk quite early and we were all laughing about the drowning of David Grenier.

I didn't say a word.

Laughing at Lalla, because Lalla nearly drowned too. You see, she was caught in a current and instead of fighting it she just relaxed and went with it out to sea and eventually came back in a semi-circle. Claimed she passed ships.

And then Trevor got up in a temper and challenged Hilden to a duel. He couldn't *stand* everyone laughing, and Hilden and Doris (your mother) being drunk, two of them flirting away he thought.

But *why?*, your mother asked Trevor.

Because he is casting aspersions on you . . .

Nonsense, I love aspersions. And everyone laughed and Trevor stood there in a rage.

And then, said Barbara, I realized that Trevor had been in love with your mother, your father always *said* there was a secret admirer. Trevor couldn't stand Hilden and her having a good time in front of him.

Nonsense, said your mother. It would have been incest. And besides (watching Hilden and Trevor and aware of the fascinated dinner table audience), both these men are after my old age pension.

What happened, said Hilden, was that I drew a line around Doris in the sand. A circle. And threatened her, "don't you dare step out of that circle or I'll thrash you."

Wait a minute, wait a minute, *when* is this happening?

Your mother is nine years old, Hilden says. And out in the sea near Negombo David Grenier is drowning. I didn't want her to go out.

You were in love with a nine year old?

Neither Hilden nor Trevor were *ever* in love with our mother, Gillian whispers to me. People always get that way at weddings, always remembering the past in a sentimental way, pretending great secret passions which went unsaid . . .

No No No. Trevor *was* in love with your mother.

Rot!

I was in my twenties, Hilden chimes in. Your mother was nine. I simply didn't want her going into the water while we tried to rescue David Grenier. Dickie, his wife, had fainted. Lalla — your mother's mother — was caught in the current and out at sea, I was on the shore with Trevor.

Trevor was there too you see.

89

Who is Hilden? asks Tory.

I am Hilden . . . your host!

Oh.

Anyway . . . there seems to be three different stories that you're telling.

No, *one*, everybody says laughing.

One when your mother was nine. Then when she was sixty-five and drinking at the wedding lunch, and obviously there is a period of unrequited love suffered by the silent Trevor who never stated his love but always fought with anyone he thought was insulting your mother, even if in truth she was simply having a good time with them the way she was with Hilden, when she was sixty-five.

Good God, I was there with them both, says Barbara, and *I'm* married to Hilden.

So where is my grandmother?

She is now out at sea while Hilden dramatically draws a circle round your mother and says "Don't you *dare* step out of that!" Your mother watches David Grenier drowning. Grenier's wife — who is going to marry three more times including one man who went crazy — is lying in the sand having fainted. And your mother can see the bob of her mother's head in the waves now and then.

Hilden and Trevor are trying to retrieve David Grenier's body, carefully, so as not to get caught in the current themselves.

My mother is nine.

Your mother is nine. And this takes place in Negombo.

OK

So an hour later my grandmother, Lalla, comes back and entertains everyone with stories of how she passed ships out there and they tell her David Grenier is dead. And nobody wants to break the news to his wife Dickie. Nobody could. And Lalla says, alright, she will, for Dickie is her sister. And she went and sat with Dickie who was still in a faint in the sand, and Lalla, wearing her elaborate bathing suit, held her hand. Don't shock her, says Trevor, whatever you do break it to her gently. My grandmother waves him away and for fifteen minutes she sits alone with her sister, waiting for her to waken. She doesn't know what to say. She is also suddenly very tired. She hates hurting anybody.

The two men, Hilden and Trevor, will walk with her daughter, my mother, about a hundred yards away down the beach, keeping their distance, waiting until they see Dickie sitting up. And then they will walk slowly back towards Dickie and my grandmother and give their sympathies.

Dickie stirs. Lalla is holding her hand. She looks up and the first words are, "How is David? Is he alright?" "Quite well, darling," Lalla says. "He is in the next room having a cup of tea."

AUNTS

How I have used them. . . .

They knit the story together, each memory a wild thread in the sarong. They lead me through their dark rooms crowded with various kinds of furniture — teak, rattan, calamander, bamboo — their voices whispering over tea, cigarettes, distracting me from the tale with their long bony arms, which move over the table like the stretched feet of storks. I would love to photograph this. The thin muscle on the upper arms, the bones and veins at the wrist that almost become part of the discreet bangle, all disappearing into the river of bright sari or faded cotton print.

My aunt Dolly stands five foot tall, weighing seventy pounds. She has not stopped smoking since the age of fifteen and her 80-year-old brain leaps like a spark plug bringing this year that year to life. Always repeating the last three words of your question and then turning a surprising corner on her own. In the large house whose wings are now disintegrating into garden and bush she moves frail as Miss Havisham. From outside the house seems incapable of use. I climb in through the window that frames her and she greets me with "I never thought I'd see you again," and suddenly all these journeys are worth it, just to be able to hug this thin woman who throws her cane onto the table in order to embrace me.

She and her brother Arthur were my father's close friends all his life. He knew that, whatever he had done, Arthur would be there to talk him out of madness, weakness, aloneness. They introduced most of the children of our generation to the theatre, dressing us up in costumes for *The Mikado*, *A Midsummer Night's Dream* — all of which Dolly made herself. Although her family was not excessive in their affairs, they shielded anyone who was in the midst of a passion. "Affairs were going on all around us, even when we were children . . . so we were well trained."

Today is one of Dolly's deaf days but the conversation rolls with the pure joy of the meeting. "Oh I looked after you several times when you were in Boralesgamuwa, do you remember?" "Yes, yes." "WHAT?" "*Yes.*" The frailty does not stop her stories though she pauses now and then to say, "God if you quote me I'm dead. I'll be caught for libel and *killed.* . . . You see they liked their flirtations. All the wives met their beaux in the Cinnamon Gardens, that's where they went to flirt, then they'd come here and use us as an alibi. Your grandmother Lalla for instance had lots of relationships. We could never keep up with her. We almost had to write the names down to remember who she was seeing. My advice you see is to get on with everybody — no matter what they do."

The conversation is continually halted by a man lying just below the ceiling hammering nails into it — hoping to keep it propped up for a few more years. Outside loud chickens fill in the spaces between Dolly's words. Eyes squint in the smoke. "I wish I could see you properly but my glasses are being fixed this week."

As I prepare to leave she walks with me, half deaf and blind, under several ladders in her living room that balance paint and workmen, into the garden where there is a wild horse, a 1930 car splayed flat on its axles and hundreds of flowering bushes so that her eyes swim out into the dark green and unfocussed purple. There is very little now that separates the house from the garden. Rain and vines and chickens move into the building. Before I leave, she points to a group photograph of a fancy dress party that shows herself and my grandmother Lalla among the crowd. She has looked at it for years and has in this way memorized everyone's place in the picture. She reels off names and laughs at the facial expressions she can no longer see. It has moved tangible, palpable, into her brain, the way memory invades the present in those who are old, the way gardens invade houses here, the way her tiny body steps into mine as intimate as anything I have witnessed and I have to force myself to be gentle with this frailty in the midst of my embrace.

THE PASSIONS
OF LALLA

 My Grandmother died in the blue arms of a jacaranda tree.
She could read thunder.

She claimed to have been born outdoors, abruptly, during a picnic, though there is little evidence for this. Her father — who came from a subdued line of Keyts — had thrown caution to the winds and married a Dickman. The bloodline was considered eccentric (one Dickman had set herself on fire) and rumours about the family often percolated across Colombo in hushed tones. "People who married the Dickmans were afraid."

There is no information about Lalla growing up. Perhaps she was a shy child, for those who are magical break from silent structures after years of chrysalis. By the time she was twenty she was living in Colombo and tentatively engaged to Shelton de Saram — a very good looking and utterly selfish man. He desired the good life, and when Frieda Donhorst arrived from England "with a thin English varnish and the Donhorst checkbook" he promptly married her. Lalla was heartbroken. She went into fits of rage, threw herself on and pounded various beds belonging to her immediate family, and quickly married Willie Gratiaen — a champion cricketer — on the rebound.

Willie was also a broker, and being one of the first Ceylonese to work for the English firm of E. John and Co. brought them most of their local business. The married couple bought a large house called "Palm Lodge" in the heart of Colombo and here, in the three acres that came with the house, they began a dairy. The dairy was Willie's second attempt at raising livestock. Fond of eggs, he had decided earlier to import and raise a breed of black chicken from Australia. At great expense the prize Australorp eggs arrived by ship, ready for hatching, but Lalla accidentally cooked them all while preparing for a dinner party.

Shortly after Willie began the dairy he fell seriously ill. Lalla, unable to cope, would run into neighbours' homes, pound on their beds, and promise to become a Catholic if Willie recovered. He never did and Lalla was left to bring up their two children.

She was not yet thirty, and for the next few years her closest friend was her neighbour, Rene de Saram, who also ran a dairy. Rene's husband disliked Lalla and disliked his wife's chickens. Lalla and the chickens would wake him before dawn every morning, especially Lalla with her loud laughter filtering across the garden as she organized the milkers. One morning Rene woke to silence and, stepping into the garden, discovered her husband tying the beaks of all the chickens with little pieces of string, or in some cases with rubber bands. She protested, but he prevailed and soon they saw their chickens perform a dance of death, dying of exhaustion and hunger, a few managing to escape along Inner

Flower Road, some kidnapped by a furious Lalla in the folds of her large brown dress and taken to Palm Lodge where she had them cooked. A year later the husband lapsed into total silence and the only sounds which could be heard from his quarters were barkings and later on the cluck of hens. It is believed he was the victim of someone's charm. For several weeks he clucked, barked, and chirped, tearing his feather pillows into snowstorms, scratching at the expensive parquet floors, leaping from first-storey windows onto the lawn. After he shot himself, Rene was left at the age of thirty-two to bring up their children. So both Rene and Lalla, after years of excessive high living, were to have difficult times — surviving on their wits and character and beauty. Both widows became the focus of the attention of numerous bored husbands. Neither of them was to marry again.

Each had thirty-five cows. Milking began at four-thirty in the morning and by six their milkmen would be cycling all over town to deliver fresh milk to customers. Lalla and Rene took the law into their own hands whenever necessary. When one of their cows caught Rinderpest Fever — a disease which could make government officials close down a dairy for months — Rene took the army pistol which had already killed her husband and personally shot it dead. With Lalla's help she burnt it and buried it in her garden. The milk went out that morning as usual, the tin vessels clanking against the handlebars of several bicycles.

Lalla's head milkman at this time was named Brumphy, and when a Scot named McKay made a pass at a servant girl Brumphy stabbed him to death. By the time the police arrived Lalla had hidden him in one of her sheds, and when they came back a second time she had taken Brumphy over to a neighbour named Lillian Bevan. For some reason Mrs. Bevan approved of everything Lalla did. She was sick when Lalla stormed in to hide Brumphy under the bed whose counterpane had wide lace edges that came down to the floor. Lalla explained that it was only a minor crime; when the police came to the Bevan household and described the brutal stabbing in graphic detail Lillian was terrified as the murderer was just a few feet away from her. But she could never disappoint Lalla and kept quiet. The police watched the house for two days and Lillian dutifully halved her meals and passed a share under the bed. "I'm proud of you darling!" said Lalla when she eventually spirited Brumphy away to another location.

However, there was a hearing in court presided over by Judge E. W. Jayawardene — one of Lalla's favourite bridge partners. When she was called to give evidence she kept referring to him as "My Lord My God." E.W. was probably one of the ugliest men in Ceylon at the time. When he asked Lalla if Brumphy was good-looking — trying humorously to suggest some motive for her protecting him — she replied, "Good looking? Who can say, My Lord My God, some people may find *you* good looking." She was thrown out of court while the gallery hooted with laughter and gave her a standing ovation. This dialogue is still in the judicial records in the Buller's Road Court Museum. In any case she continued to play bridge with E. W. Jayawardene and their sons would remain close friends.

Apart from rare appearances in court (sometimes to watch other friends give evidence), Lalla's day was carefully planned. She would be up at four with the milkers, oversee the dairy, look after the books, and be finished by 9 A.M. The rest of the day would be given over to gallivanting — social calls, lunch parties, visits from admirers, and bridge. She also brought up her two children. It was in the garden at Palm Lodge that my mother and Dorothy

Clementi-Smith would practise their dances, quite often surrounded by cattle.

*   *   *

For years Palm Lodge attracted a constant group — first as children, then teenagers, and then young adults. For most of her life children flocked to Lalla, for she was the most casual and irresponsible of chaperones, being far too busy with her own life to oversee them all. Behind Palm Lodge was a paddy field which separated her house from "Royden," where the Daniels lived. When there were complaints that hordes of children ran into Royden with muddy feet, Lalla bought ten pairs of stilts and taught them to walk across the paddy fields on these "borukakuls" or "lying legs." Lalla would say "yes" to any request if she was busy at bridge so they knew when to ask her for permission to do the most outrageous things. Every child had to be part of the group. She particularly objected to children being sent for extra tuition on Saturdays and would hire a Wallace Carriage and go searching for children like Peggy Peiris. She swept into the school at noon yelling "PEGGY!!!," fluttering down the halls in her long black clothes loose at the edges like a rooster dragging its tail, and Peggy's friends would lean over the banisters and say "Look, look, your mad aunt has arrived."

As these children grew older they discovered that Lalla had very little money. She would take groups out for meals and be refused service as she hadn't paid her previous bills. Everyone went with her anyway, though they could never be sure of eating. It was the same with adults. During one of her grand dinner parties she asked Lionel Wendt who was very shy to carve the meat. A big pot was placed in front of him. As he removed the lid a baby goat jumped out and skittered down the table. Lalla had been so involved with the joke — buying the kid that morning and finding a big enough pot — that she had forgotten about the real dinner and there was nothing to eat once the shock and laughter had subsided.

In the early years her two children, Noel and Doris, could hardly move without being used as part of Lalla's daily theatre. She was constantly dreaming up costumes for my mother to wear to fancy dress parties, which were the rage at the time. Because of Lalla, my mother won every fancy dress competition for three years while in her late teens. Lalla tended to go in for animals or sea creatures. The crowning achievement was my mother's appearance at the Galle Face Dance as a lobster — the outfit bright red and covered with crustaceans and claws which grew out of her shoulder blades and seemed to move of their own accord. The problem was that she could not sit down for the whole evening but had to walk or waltz stiffly from side to side with her various beaux who, although respecting the imagination behind the outfit, found her beautiful frame almost unapproachable. Who knows, this may have been Lalla's ulterior motive. For years my mother tended to be admired from a distance. On the ballroom floor she stood out in her animal or shell fish beauty but claws and caterpillar bulges tended to deflect suitors from thoughts of seduction. When couples paired off to walk along Galle Face Green under the moonlight it would, after all, be embarrassing to be seen escorting a lobster.

When my mother eventually announced her engagement to my father, Lalla turned to friends and said, "What do you *think*, darling, she's going to marry an Ondaatje . . . she's going to marry a *Tamil!*" Years later, when I sent my mother my first book of poems, she met my sister at the door with a shocked face and in exactly the same tone and phrasing said, "What do you *think*, Janet" (her hand holding her cheek to emphasize the tragedy), "Michael has become a *poet!*" Lalla continued to stress the Tamil element in my father's background, which pleased him enormously. For the wedding ceremony she had two marriage chairs decorated in a Hindu style and laughed all through the ceremony. The incident was, however, the beginning of a war with my father.

Eccentrics can be the most irritating people to live with. My mother, for instance, strangely, *never* spoke of Lalla to me. Lalla was loved most by people who saw her arriving from the distance like a storm. She did love children, or at least loved company of any kind — cows, adults, babies, dogs. She always had to be surrounded. But being "grabbed" or "contained" by anyone drove her mad. She would be compassionate to the character of children but tended to avoid holding them on her lap. And she could not abide having grandchildren hold her hands when she took them for walks. She would quickly divert them into the entrance of the frightening maze in the Nuwara Eliya Park and leave them there, lost, while she went off to steal flowers. She was always determined to be physically selfish. Into her sixties she would still complain of how she used to be "pinned down" to breast feed her son before she could leave for dances.

* * *

With children grown up and out of the way, Lalla busied herself with her sisters and brothers. "Dickie" seemed to be marrying constantly; after David Grenier drowned she married a de Vos, a Wombeck, and then an Englishman. Lalla's brother Vere attempted to remain a bachelor all his life. When she was flirting with Catholicism she decided that Vere should marry her priest's sister — a woman who *had* planned on becoming a nun. The sister also had a dowry of thirty thousand rupees, and both Lalla and Vere were short of money at the time, for both enjoyed expensive drinking sessions. Lalla masterminded the marriage, even though the woman wasn't good-looking and Vere liked good-looking women. On the wedding night the bride prayed for half an hour beside the bed and then started singing hymns, so Vere departed, forgoing nuptial bliss, and for the rest of her life the poor woman had a sign above her door which read "Unloved. Unloved. Unloved." Lalla went to mass the following week, having eaten a huge meal. When refused mass she said, "Then I'll resign," and avoided the church for the rest of her life.

A good many of my relatives from this generation seem to have tormented the church sexually. Italian monks who became enamoured of certain aunts would return to Italy to discard their robes and return to find the women already married. Jesuit fathers too were falling out of the church and into love with the de Sarams with the regularity of mangoes thudding onto dry lawns during a drought. Vere also became the concern of various religious groups that tried to save him. And during the last months of his life he was "held captive" by a group of Roman Catholic nuns in Galle so that no one knew where he was until the announcement of his death.

Vere was known as "a sweet drunk" and he and Lalla always drank together. While Lalla grew loud and cheerful, Vere became excessively courteous. Drink was hazardous for him, however, as he came to believe he escaped the laws of gravity while under the influence. He kept trying to hang his hat on walls where there was no hook and often stepped out of boats to walk home. But drink quietened him except for these few excesses. His close friend, the lawyer Cox Sproule, was a different matter. Cox was charming when sober and brilliant when drunk. He would appear in court stumbling over chairs with a mind clear as a bell, winning cases under a judge who had pleaded with him just that morning not to appear in court in such a condition. He hated the English. Unlike Cox, Vere had no profession to focus whatever talents he had. He did try to become an auctioneer but being both shy and drunk he was a failure. The only job that came his way was supervising Italian prisoners during the war. Once a week he would ride to Colombo on his motorcycle, bringing as many bottles of alcohol as he could manage for his friends and his sister. He had encouraged the prisoners to set up a brewery, so that there was a distillery in every hut in the prison camp. He remained drunk with the prisoners for most of the war years. Even Cox Sproule joined him for six months when he was jailed for helping three German spies escape from the country.

What happened to Lalla's other brother, Evan, no one knows. But all through her life, when the children sent her money, Lalla would immediately forward it on to Evan. He was supposedly a thief and Lalla loved him. "Jesus died to save sinners," she said, "and I will die for Evan." Evan manages to escape family memory, appearing only now and then to offer blocs of votes to any friend running for public office by bringing along all his illegitimate children.

* * *

By the mid-thirties both Lalla's and Rene's dairies had been wiped out by Rinderpest. Both were drinking heavily and both were broke.

We now enter the phase when Lalla is best remembered. Her children were married and out of the way. Most of her social life had been based at Palm Lodge but now she had to sell the house, and she burst loose on the country and her friends like an ancient monarch who had lost all her possessions. She was free to move wherever she wished, to do whatever she wanted. She took thorough advantage of everyone and had bases all over the country. Her schemes for organizing parties and bridge games exaggerated themselves. She was full of the "passions," whether drunk or not. She had always loved flowers but in her last decade couldn't be bothered to grow them. Still, whenever she arrived on a visit she would be carrying an armful of flowers and announce, "Darling, I've just been to church and I've stolen some flowers for you. These are from Mrs. Abeysekare's, the lilies are from Mrs. Ratnayake's, the agapanthus is from Violet Meedeniya, and the rest are from *your* garden." She stole flowers compulsively, even in the owner's presence. As she spoke with someone her straying left hand would pull up a prize rose along with the roots, all so that she could appreciate it for that one moment, gaze into it with complete pleasure, swallow its qualities whole, and then hand the flower, discarding it, to the owner. She ravaged some of the best gardens in Colombo and Nuwara Eliya. For some years she was barred from the Hakgalle Public Gardens.

Property was there to be taken or given away. When she was rich she had given parties for all the poor children in the neighbourhood and handed out gifts. When she was poor she still organized them but now would go out to the Pettah market on the morning of the party and steal toys. All her life she had given away everything she owned to whoever wanted it and so now felt free to take whatever she wanted. She was a lyrical socialist. Having no home in her last years, she breezed into houses for weekends or even weeks, cheated at bridge with her closest friends, calling them "damn thieves," "bloody rogues." She only played cards for money and if faced with a difficult contract would throw down her hand, gather the others up, and proclaim "the rest are mine." Everyone knew she was lying but it didn't matter. Once when my brother and two sisters who were very young were playing a game of "beggar-my-neighbour" on the porch, Lalla came to watch. She walked up and down beside them, seemingly very irritated. After ten minutes she could stand it no longer, opened her purse, gave them each two rupees, and said, "Never, *never* play cards for love."

She was in her prime. During the war she opened up a boarding house in Nuwara Eliya with Muriel Potger, a chain smoker who did all the work while Lalla breezed through the rooms saying, "Muriel, for godsake, we can't breathe in this place!"— being more of a pest than a help. If she had to go out she would say, "I'll just freshen up" and disappear into her room for a stiff drink. If there was none she took a quick swig of eau de cologne to snap her awake. Old flames visited her constantly throughout her life. She refused to lose friends; even her first beau, Shelton de Saram, would arrive after breakfast to escort her for walks. His unfortunate wife, Frieda, would always telephone Lalla first and would spend most afternoons riding in her trap through the Cinnamon Gardens or the park searching for them.

Lalla's great claim to fame was that she was the first woman in Ceylon to have a mastectomy. It turned out to be unnecessary but she always claimed to support modern science, throwing herself into new causes. (Even in death her generosity exceeded the physically possible for she had donated her body to six hospitals.) The false breast would never be still for long. She was an energetic person. It would crawl over to join its twin on the right hand side or sometimes appear on her back, "for dancing" she smirked. She called it her Wandering Jew and would yell at the grandchildren in the middle of a formal dinner to fetch her tit as she had forgotten to put it on. She kept losing the contraption to servants who were mystified by it as well as to the dog, Chindit, who would be found gnawing at the foam as if it were tender chicken. She went through four breasts in her lifetime. One she left on a branch of a tree in Hakgalle Gardens to dry out after a rainstorm, one flew off when she was riding behind Vere on his motorbike, and the third she was very mysterious about, almost embarrassed though Lalla was never embarrassed. Most believed it had been forgotten after a romantic assignation in Trincomalee with a man who may or may not have been in the Cabinet.

*   *   *

Children tell little more than animals, said Kipling. When Lalla came to Bishop's College Girls School on Parents' Day and pissed behind bushes — or when in Nuwara Eliya she simply stood with her legs apart and urinated — my sisters were so embarrassed and ashamed they did not admit or speak of this to each other for over fifteen years. Lalla's son Noel was most appalled by her. She, however, was immensely proud of his success, and my Aunt Nedra recalls seeing Lalla sitting on a sack of rice in the fish market surrounded by workers and fishermen, with whom she was having one of her long daily chats, pointing to a picture of a bewigged judge in *The Daily News* and saying in Sinhalese that *this* was *her* son. But Lalla could never be just a mother; that seemed to be only one muscle in her chameleon nature, which had too many other things to reflect. And I am not sure what my mother's relationship was to her. Maybe they were too similar to even recognize much of a problem, both having huge compassionate hearts that never even considered revenge or small-mindedness, both howling and wheezing with laughter over the frailest joke, both carrying their own theatre on their backs. Lalla remained the centre of the world she moved through. She had been beautiful when young but most free after her husband died and her children grew up. There was some sense of divine right she felt she and everyone else had, even if she had to beg for it or steal it. This overbearing charmed flower.

*　*　*

In her last years she was searching for the great death. She never found, looking under leaves, the giant snake, the fang which would brush against the ankle like a whisper. A whole generation grew old or died around her. Prime Ministers fell off horses, a jellyfish slid down the throat of a famous swimmer. During the forties she moved with the rest of the country towards Independence and the 20th century. Her freedom accelerated. Her arms still flagged down strange cars for a lift to the Pettah market where she could trade gossip with her friends and place bets in the "bucket shops." She carried everything she really needed with her, and a friend meeting her once at a train station was appalled to be given as a gift a huge fish that Lalla had carried doubled up in her handbag.

She could be silent as a snake or flower. She loved the thunder; it spoke to her like a king. As if her mild dead husband had been transformed into a cosmic umpire, given the megaphone of nature. Sky noises and the abrupt light told her details of careers, incidental wisdom, allowing her to risk everything because the thunder would warn her along with the snake of lightning. She would stop the car and swim in the Mahaveli, serene among currents, still wearing her hat. Would step out of the river, dry in the sun for five minutes and climb back into the car among the shocked eyeballs of her companions, her huge handbag once more on her lap carrying four packs of cards, possibly a fish.

In August 1947, she received a small inheritance, called her brother Vere, and they drove off to Nuwara Eliya on his motorcycle. She was 68 years old. These were to be her last days. The boarding house she had looked after during the war was empty and so they bought food and booze and moved in to play "Ajoutha"— a card game that normally takes at least eight hours. It was a game the Portuguese had taught the Sinhalese in the 15th century to keep them quiet and preoccupied while they invaded the country. Lalla opened the bottles of Rocklands Gin (the same brand that was destroying her son-in-law) and Vere prepared the Italian menus, which he had learned from his prisoners of war. In her earlier days in Nuwara Eliya, Lalla would have been up at dawn to walk through the park — inhabited at that hour only by nuns and monkeys — walk round the golf-course where gardeners would stagger under the weight of giant python-like hoses as they watered the greens. But now she slept till noon, and in the early evening rode up to Moon Plains, her arms spread out like a crucifix behind Vere.

Moon Plains. Drowned in blue and gold flowers whose names she had never bothered to learn, tugged by the wind, leaning in angles for miles and miles against the hills 5000 feet above sea level. They watched the exit of the sun and the sudden appearance of the moon half way up the sky. Those lovely accidental moons — a horn a chalice a thumbnail — and then they would climb onto the motorcycle, the 60-year-old brother and the 68-year-old sister, who was his best friend forever.

Riding back on August 13, 1947, they heard the wild thunder and she knew someone was going to die. Death, however, not to be read out there. She gazed and listened but there seemed to be no victim or parabola end beyond her. It rained hard during the last mile to the house and they went indoors to drink for the rest of the evening. The next day the rains continued and she refused Vere's offer of a ride knowing there would be death soon. "Cannot wreck this perfect body, Vere. The police will spend hours searching for my breast thinking it was lost in the crash." So they played two-handed Ajoutha and drank. But now she could not sleep at all, and they talked as they never had about husbands, lovers, his various possible marriages. She did not mention her readings of the thunder to Vere, who was now almost comatose on the bluebird print sofa. But she could not keep her eyes closed like him and at 5 A.M. on August 15, 1947, she wanted fresh air, needed to walk, a walk to Moon Plains, no motorcycle, no danger, and she stepped out towards the still dark night of almost dawn and straight into the floods.

For two days and nights they had been oblivious to the amount of destruction outside their home. The whole country was mauled by the rains that year. Ratmalana, Bentota, Chilaw, Anuradhapura, were all under water. The forty-foot-high Peradeniya Bridge had been swept away. In Nuwara Eliya, Galways's Land Bird Sanctuary and the Golf Course were ten feet under water. Snakes and fish from the lake swam into the windows of the Golf Club, into the bar, and around the indoor badminton court. Fish were found captured in the badminton nets when the flood receded a week later. Lalla took one step off the front porch and was immediately hauled away by an arm of water, her handbag bursting open. 208 cards moved ahead of her like a disturbed nest as she was thrown downhill still comfortable and drunk, snagged for a few moments on the railings of the Good Shepherd Convent and then lifted away towards the town of Nuwara Eliya.

It was her last perfect journey. The new river in the street moved her right across the race course and park towards the bus station. As the light came up slowly she was being swirled fast, "floating" (as ever confident of surviving this too) alongside branches and leaves, the dawn starting to hit flamboyant trees as she slipped past them like a dark log, shoes lost, false breast lost. She was free as a fish, travelling faster than she had in years, fast as Vere's motor-cycle, only now there was this *roar* around her. She overtook Jesus lizards that swam and ran in bursts over the water, she was sur-rounded by tired half-drowned fly-catchers screaming *tack tack tack tack*, frogmouths, nightjars forced to keep awake, brain-fever birds and their irritating ascending scales, snake eagles, scimitar-babblers, they rode the air around Lalla wishing to perch on her unable to alight on anything except what was moving.

What was moving was rushing flood. In the park she floated over the intricate fir tree hedges of the maze — which would always continue to terrify her grandchildren — its secret spread out naked as a skeleton for her. The symmetrical flower beds also began to receive the day's light and Lalla gazed down at them with wonder, moving as lazily as that long dark scarf which trailed off her neck brushing the branches and never catching. She would always wear silk, as she showed us, her grandchildren, would pull the scarf like a fluid through the ring removed from her finger, pulled sleepily through, as she moved now, awake to the new angle of her favourite trees, the Syzygium, the Araucaria Pine, over the now unnecessary iron gates of the park, and through the town of Nuwara Eliya itself and its shops and stalls where she had haggled for guavas, now six feet under water, windows smashed in by the weight of all this collected rain.

Drifting slower she tried to hold onto things. A bicycle hit her across the knees. She saw the dead body of a human. She began to see the drowned dogs of the town. Cattle. She saw men on roofs fighting with each other, looting, almost surprised by the quick dawn in the mountains revealing them, not even watching her magic ride, the alcohol still in her — serene and relaxed.

Below the main street of Nuwara Eliya the land drops suddenly and Lalla fell into deeper waters, past the houses of "Cranleigh" and "Ferncliff." They were homes she knew well, where she had played and argued over cards. The water here was rougher and she went under for longer and longer moments coming up with a gasp and then pulled down like bait, pulled under by some-thing not comfortable any more, and then there was the great blue ahead of her, like a sheaf of blue wheat, like a large eye that peered towards her, and she hit it and was dead.

THE
PRODIGAL

HARBOUR

I arrived in a plane but love the harbour. Dusk. And the turning on of electricity in ships, portholes of moon, the blue glide of a tug, the harbour road and its ship chandlers, soap makers, ice on bicycles, the hidden anonymous barber shops behind the pink dirt walls of Reclamation Street.

One frail memory dragged up out of the past — going to the harbour to say goodbye to a sister or mother, dusk. For years I loved the song, "Harbour lights," and later in my teens danced disgracefully with girls, humming "Sea of Heartbreak."

There is nothing wise about a harbour, but it is real life. It is as sincere as a Singapore cassette. Infinite waters cohabit with flotsam on this side of the breakwater and the luxury liners and Maldive fishing vessels steam out to erase calm sea. Who was I saying goodbye to? Automatically as I travel on the tug with my brother-in-law, a pilot in the harbour, I sing "the lights in the harbour don't shine for me . . ." but I love it here, skimming out into the night anonymous among the lazy commerce, my nieces dancing on the breakwater as they wait, the lovely swallowing of thick night air as it carves around my brain, blunt, cleaning itself with nothing but this anonymity, with the magic words. *Harbour. Lost ship. Chandler. Estuary.*

MONSOON
NOTEBOOK (ii)

The bars across the windows did not always work. When bats would invade the house at dusk, the beautiful long-haired girls would rush to the corner of rooms and hide their heads under dresses. The bats suddenly drifting like dark squadrons through the house — for never more than two minutes — arcing into the halls over the uncleared dining room table and out along the verandah where the parents would be sitting trying to capture the cricket scores on the BBC with a shortwave radio.

Wildlife stormed or crept into homes this way. The snake either entered through the bathroom drain for remnants of water or, finding the porch doors open, came in like a king and moved in a straight line through the living room, dining room, the kitchen and servant's quarters, and out the back, as if taking the most civilized short cut to another street in town. Others moved in permanently; birds nested above the fans, the silverfish slid into steamer trunks and photograph albums — eating their way through portraits and wedding pictures. What images of family life they consumed in their minute jaws and took into their bodies no thicker than the pages they ate.

And the animals also on the periphery of rooms and porches, their sounds forever in your ear. During our visit to the jungle, while we slept on the verandah at 3 A.M., night would be suddenly alive with disturbed peacocks. A casual movement from one of them roosting in the trees would waken them all and, so fussing, sounding like branches full of cats, they would weep weep loud into the night.

One evening I kept the tape recorder beside my bed and wakened by them once more out of a deep sleep automatically pressed the machine on to record them. Now, and here, Canadian February, I write this in the kitchen and play that section of cassette to hear not just peacocks but all the noises of the night behind them — inaudible then because they were always there like breath. In this silent room (with its own unheard hum of fridge, fluorescent light) there are these frogs loud as river, gruntings, the whistle of other birds brash and sleepy, but in that night so modest behind the peacocks they were unfocussed by the brain — nothing more than darkness, all those sweet loud younger brothers of the night.

HOW I WAS BATHED

We are having a formal dinner. String hoppers, meat
curry, egg rulang, papadams, potato curry. Alice's date chutney,
seeni sambol, mallung and brinjals and iced water. All the dishes
are on the table and a good part of the meal is spent passing them
around to each other. It is my favourite meal — anything that has
string hoppers and egg rulang I eat with a lascivious hunger. For
dessert there is buffalo curd and jaggery sauce — a sweet honey
made from the coconut, like maple syrup but with a smoky taste.

In this formal setting Gillian begins to describe to everyone
present how I used to be bathed when I was five. She had heard
the story in detail from Yasmine Gooneratne, who was a prefect
with her at Bishop's College for Girls. I listen intently, making
sure I get a good portion of the egg rulang.

The first school I went to was a girls' school in Colombo which
accepted young boys of five or six for a couple of years. The nurse

or ayah in charge of our cleanliness was a small, muscular and vicious woman named Maratina. I roamed with my pack of school friends, usually filthy from morning to night, and every second evening we were given a bath. The bathroom was a sparse empty stone room with open drains in the floor and a tap to one side. We were marched in by Maratina and ordered to strip. She collected our clothes, threw them out of the room, and locked the door. The eight of us were herded terrified into one corner.

Maratina filled a bucket with water and flung the contents towards our cowering screaming bodies. Another bucket was filled and hurled towards us hard as a police hose. Then she strode forward, grabbed a child by the hair, pulled him over to the centre, scrubbed him violently with carbolic soap and threw him towards the opposite side of the room. She plucked another and repeated the soaping. Totally in control of the squirming bodies, she eventually scrubbed us all, then returned to the bucket and thrashed water over our soapy nakedness. Bleary-eyed, our bodies tingling and reeling, our hair curved back from the force of the throw, we stood there shining. She approached with a towel, dried us fast and brutally, and threw us out one by one to get into our sarongs and go to bed.

The guests, the children, everyone is laughing and Gillian is no doubt exaggerating Yasmine's account in her usual style, her long arms miming the capture and scrub of five-year-olds. I am dreaming and wondering why this was never to be traumatically remembered. It is the kind of event that should have surfaced as the first chapter of an anguished autobiographical novel. I am thinking also of Yasmine Gooneratne, now teaching at a university in Australia, whom I met just last year at an International Writers' Conference in New Delhi. We talked then mostly about

Gillian who had also been at university with her. Why did *she* not tell me the story — this demure woman in a sari who was once "bath prefect" at Bishop's College Girl's School, who officiated over the cleansing of my lean five-year-old nakedness?

WILPATTU

April 8th

From Anuradhapura we
drive towards the Wilpattu Jungle, through the small town of
Nochiyagama. "That's it," I tell my daughter, "that'll be a good
name for a child of yours." *Nochi.* Once we reach Wilpattu a tracker-
guide is assigned to us. He will live with us during the next few
days and be with us whenever we take treks out in the jeep to look
for animals. We now have an hour's journey to the middle of the
jungle. It is a slow ten-mile-an-hour drive on bad roads of red
clay and sand.

5 P.M. Manikappolu Utu. A large wooden house on stilts, and
fresh "elephant droppings" around the place, which turn out to be
buffalo shit. We empty the jeep of all the food we have brought
and begin to change out of sweat-soaked clothes. On the porch
is a muted light and long cane chairs. A delicate rain begins pat-
tering on the tin roof then suddenly veers into a thunder shower

which whitens the landscape. To the left of the house is a huge pond, almost a lake, where water lilies float closed at this hour, now being pounded bouncing under the rain. The girls are out there in their dresses getting wet and suddenly the rest of us decide this is the only chance for a bath that we will have here and walk out into the storm. Nine of us holding up our arms for all the rain we can reach.

We are slightly drunk with this place — the beautiful house, the animals which are appearing now, and this tough cold rain turning the hard-baked earth into red mud. All of us are in our solitude. Not really concerned about the others, just revelling in a private pleasure. It is like communal sleep. The storm falters then starts up again, wilder than ever. The bungalow's cook and the tracker watch from the doorways of the house not quite believing what is happening to this strange mixture of people — Sinhalese, Canadian, and one quiet French girl — who are now soaping themselves with a bar of soap and throwing it around like a foaming elixir so everyone is suddenly white, as if in a petticoat, and now trying even harder to catch the rain everywhere, bending over to let it land on our backs and shoulders. Some move under the warmer rain of the trees, some sit as if it was Sunday afternoon on a bench by the pond of water lilies and crocodiles, and the others wade ankle-deep in swirling mud by the jeep. On the other side of the pond there are about thirty deer — as if in a dry universe. And storks on the bank whose reflections are being shattered.

Then a new burst of energy. A *val oora* — a large filthy black wild boar has appeared majestically out of the trees with tusks that turn his quiet face into hair-lipped deformity. He watches, making us aware of each other half-soaped, happy and ridiculous, dresses heavy with rain, sarongs above the knees. All of us — the

123

lilies, the trees with their wind drunk hair, this magnificent val oora who is now the centre of the storm — celebrating the elimination of heat. He moves straight-thighed, stiff, but with a lunging walk, keeping his polite distance.

Wild black pig in a white rainstorm, concerned about this invasion, this metamorphosis of soap, this dented Volkswagen, this jeep. He can take his pick, any one of us. If I am to die soon I would choose to die now under his wet alphabet of tusk, while I am cool and clean and in good company.

*   *   *

April 11th

Last morning in Wilpattu. Everyone packing and arguing in the hushed early light. Where is the torch? My Leyden shirt? Whose towel is this? Last night, right off the porch, a leopard tracked and waited for a chance to pounce on one of the deer that stayed around the house. Our dinner was interrupted by screams from the deer, and we were soon all outside using the flashlights to pick out the red eye of the leopard, the green eyes of the deer and later the red eye of the crocodile who had come to watch. Everyone lasciviously waiting for a kill.

Once, when there was nobody staying in this bungalow except the cook, a leopard paced up and down the porch. This is the porch onto which we have moved all the beds and slept these last three nights, telling each other ghost stories and feeling absolutely secure in the jungle heat. At one of the other bungalows guests have to sleep behind closed doors, for a bear comes regularly each night, climbs the stairs slowly as if exhausted, and sleeps on whatever free bed is available.

On this last morning I leave the others and go downstairs to find my soap which I left on a railing after one of our rain baths. It has rained every day from five thirty until six, hard perfect thunderstorms. No sign of the soap. I ask the cook and the tracker and they both give the same answer. The wild pig has taken it. *My* wild pig. That repulsively exotic creature in his thick black body and the ridge of non-symmetrical hair running down his back. This thing has walked off with my bar of Pears Transparent Soap? Why not my copy of Rumi poetry? Or Merwin translations? That soap was aristocratic and kept me feeling good all through the filthy hotels of Africa, whenever I could find a shower. The tracker and cook keep giving me evidence that it is the pig. He constantly removes things after taking a small bite, once even took a handbag. As the pig comes to the back door for garbage daily I am beginning to believe them. What does this wild pig want soap for? Visions begin to form of the creature returning to his friends with Pears Transparent Soap and then all of them bathing and scrubbing their armpits in the rain in a foul parody of us. I can see their mouths open to catch drops of water on their tongues, washing their hooves, standing complacently under the drain spout, and then moving in Pears fragrance to a dinner of Manikappolu garbage.

With me irritated at this loss we leave Wilpattu, the jeep following the Volkswagen. My eyes are peeled for a last sight of the oora, my soap caught in his tusk and his mouth foaming.

KUTTAPITIYA

The last estate we lived on as children was called Kuttapitiya and was famous for its gardens. Walls of flowers —. ochre, lavender, pink — would flourish and die within a month, followed by even more exaggerated and inbred colours. My father was superintendent of a tea and rubber plantation and each morning at 5 A.M. a drummer began his slow rhythmic beat, an alarm clock for all those who worked there. He played for half an hour and slowly and lazily we rose into the pale blue mornings. At breakfast we could watch the flamboyant tree and lavender-cotton catch fire. House and garden were perched high above the mist which filled the valley below like a mattress, cutting us off from the real world. My mother and father lived there for the longest period of their marriage.

Looking down off the edge of the garden we could see the road to Pelmadulla wind and disappear like a lethargic dark yellow snake into overhanging foliage. Everything seemed green below us. Where we stood, the muted purple leaves of orchid fell at the gentlest breeze onto someone's shadow. It was the perfect place for children who were allowed to go wild. My brother borrowing a pakispetti box, attaching wheels, and bumping down the steep slopes — a dangerous training for his future bobsledding. Having our hair cut on the front lawn by a travelling barber. And daily arguments over Monopoly, cricket, or marital issues that blazed and died on the privacy of this mountain.

And there was Lalla too, like a bee attracted to the perfume of any flower, who came up every other week solely to ransack the garden and who departed with a car full of sprigs and branches. With hardly any room to move or stretch, she rode back to Colombo, still as a corpse in a flower-packed hearse.

In his last years my father was a founding member of "The Ceylon Cactus and Succulent Society" and this interest began during his time in Kuttapitiya — all because of his devious and defensive nature. He loved ordered gardens and hated to see beds ravaged by Lalla's plundering. Gradually the vegetation at Kuttapitiya took on a prickly character. He began with roses, then Lalla wore gloves, and so he progressed to the cactus. The landscape turned grey around us. He welcomed the thorn bush, experimented with gnarled Japanese fig trees, retreated to pragmatic vegetables or spears of the succulent. His appreciation of growing things became more subtle, turned within a more limited spectrum and gradually Lalla's visits tapered away. Her journeys were in any case made solely for the effect of arriving at friends' houses in Colombo bearing soft rain-grown flowers.

This left the family alone once more. We had everything. It was and still is the most beautiful place in the world. We drove up, my family, Gillian's family, from the south coast, dusty, with headaches, tired, up a terrible stone broken road and stopped at the big bungalow. And my daughter turned to me on the edge of the lawn where I had my first haircuts and said, "If we lived here it would be perfect." "Yes," I said.

TRAVELS IN CEYLON

Ceylon falls on a map and its outline is the shape of a tear. After the spaces of India and Canada it is so small. A miniature. Drive ten miles and you are in a landscape so different that by rights it should belong to another country. From Galle in the south to Colombo a third of the way up the coast is only seventy miles. When houses were built along the coastal road it was said that a chicken could walk between the two cities without touching ground. The country is cross-hatched with maze-like routes whose only escape is the sea. From a ship or plane you can turn back or look down at the disorder. Villages spill onto streets, the jungle encroaches on village.

The Ceylon Road and Rail Map resembles a small garden full of darting red and black birds. In the middle of the 19th century, a 17-year-old English officer was ordered to organize the building of a road from Colombo to Kandy. Workers tore paths out of the sides of mountains and hacked through jungle, even drilled a huge hole through a rock on the hairpin bend of the Kadugannawa Pass. It was finished when the officer was thirty-six. There was a lot of this sort of casual obsession going on at that time.

My father, too, seemed fated to have an obsession with trains all his life. Rail trips became his nemesis. If one was to be blind drunk in the twenties and thirties, one somehow managed it on public transport, or on roads that would terrify a sober man with mountain passes, rock cuts, and precipices. Being an officer in the Ceylon Light Infantry, my father was allowed free train passes and became notorious on the Colombo-Trincomalee run.

He began quietly enough. In his twenties he pulled out his army pistol, terrified a fellow officer — John Kotelawela — under his seat, walked through the swaying carriages and threatened to kill the driver unless he stopped the train. The train halted ten miles out of Colombo at seven-thirty in the morning. He explained that he expected this trip to be a pleasant one and he wanted his good friend Arthur van Langenberg who had missed the train to enjoy it with him.

The passengers emptied out to wait on the tracks while a runner was sent back to Colombo to get Arthur. After a two-hour delay Arthur arrived, John Kotelawela came out from under his seat, everyone jumped back on, my father put his pistol away, and the train continued on to Trincomalee.

I think my father believed that he owned the railway by birth-right. He wore the railway as if it was a public suit of clothes. Trains in Ceylon lack privacy entirely. There are no individual compartments, and most of the passengers spend their time walking through carriages, curious to see who else is on board. So people usually knew when Mervyn Ondaatje boarded the train, with or without his army revolver. (He tended to stop trains more often when in uniform.) If the trip coincided with his days of dipso-mania the train could be delayed for hours. Messages would be telegraphed from one station to another to arrange for a relative to meet and remove him from the train. My uncle Noel was usually called. As he was in the Navy during the war, a naval jeep would roar towards Anuradhapura to pick up the major from the Ceylon Light Infantry.

When my father removed all his clothes and leapt from the train, rushing into the Kadugannawa tunnel, the Navy finally refused to follow and my mother was sent for. He stayed in the darkness of that three-quarter-mile-long tunnel for three hours stopping rail traffic going both ways. My mother, clutching a suit of civilian clothing (the Army would not allow her to advertise his military connections), walked into that darkness, finding him and talking with him for over an hour and a half. A moment only Conrad could have interpreted. She went in there alone, his clothes in one arm — but no shoes, an oversight he later complained of — and a railway lantern that he shattered as soon as she reached him. They had been married for six years.

They survived that darkness. And my mother, the lover of Tennyson and early Yeats, began to realize that she had caught onto a different breed of dog. She was to become tough and valiant in a very different world from then on, determined, when they divorced, never to ask him for money, and to raise us all on her own earnings. They were both from gracious, genteel fam-ilies, but my father went down a path unknown to his parents and wife. She followed him and coped with him for fourteen years, surrounding his behaviour like a tough and demure breeze. Talk-ing him out of suicide in a three-quarter-mile-long tunnel, for god's sake! She walked in armed with clothes she had borrowed from another passenger, and a light, and her knowledgeable love of all the beautiful formal poetry that existed up to the 1930s, to meet her naked husband in the darkness, in the black slow breeze of the Kadugannawa tunnel, unable to find him until he rushed at her, grabbed that lantern and dashed it against the wall before he realized who it was, who had come for him.

"It's me!"

Then a pause. And, "How *dare* you follow me!"

"I followed you because no one else would follow you."

If you look at my mother's handwriting from the thirties on, it has changed a good deal from her youth. It looks wild, drunk, the letters are much larger and billow over the pages, almost as if she had changed hands. Reading her letters we thought that the blue aerograms were written in ten seconds flat. But once my sister saw her writing and it was the most laboured process, her tongue twisting in her mouth. As if that scrawl was the result of great discipline, as if at the age of thirty or so she had been blasted, forgotten how to write, lost the use of a habitual style and forced herself to cope with a new dark unknown alphabet.

* * *

Resthouses are an old tradition in Ceylon. The roads are so dangerous that there is one every fifteen miles. You can drive in to relax, have a drink or lunch or get a room for the night. Between Colombo and Kandy people stop at the Kegalle resthouse; from Colombo to Hatton, they stop at the Kitulgala resthouse. This was my father's favourite.

It was on his travels by road that my father waged war with a certain Sammy Dias Bandaranaike, a close relative of the eventual Prime Minister of Ceylon who was assassinated by a Buddhist monk.

It is important to understand the tradition of the Visitors' Book. After a brief or long stay at a resthouse, one is expected to write one's comments. The Bandaranaike-Ondaatje feud began and was contained within the arena of such visitors' books. What happened was that Sammy Dias Bandaranaike and my father happened to visit the Kitulgala resthouse simultaneously. Sammy Dias, or so my side of the feud tells it, was a scrounger for complaints. While most people wrote two or three curt lines, he would have spent his whole visit checking every tap and shower to see what was wrong and would have plenty to say. On this occasion, Sammy left first, having written half a page in the Kitulgala resthouse visitors' book. He bitched at everything, from the service to the badly made drinks, to the poor rice, to the bad beds. Almost an epic. My father left two hours later and wrote two sentences, "No complaints. Not even about Mr. Bandaranaike." As most people read these comments, they were as public as a newspaper advertisement, and soon everyone including Sammy had heard about it. And everyone but Sammy was amused.

A few months later they both happened to hit the resthouse in Avissawella for lunch. They stayed there only an hour ignoring each other. Sammy left first, wrote a half-page attack on my father, and complimented the good food. My father wrote one and a half pages of vindictive prose about the Bandaranaike family, dropping hints of madness and incest. The next time they came together, Sammy Dias allowed my father to write first and, after he had left, put down all the gossip he knew about the Ondaatjes.

This literary war broke so many codes that for the first time in Ceylon history pages had to be ripped out of visitors' books. Eventually one would write about the other even when the other was nowhere near the resthouse. Pages continued to be torn out, ruining a good archival history of two semi-prominent Ceylon families. The war petered out when neither Sammy Dias nor my father was allowed to write their impressions of a stay or a meal. The standard comment on visitors' books today about "constructive criticism" dates from this period.

* * *

My father's last train ride (he was banned from the Ceylon Railways after 1943) was his most dramatic. The year I was born he was a major with the Ceylon Light Infantry and was stationed away from my mother in Trincomalee. There were fears of a Japanese attack and he became obsessed with a possible invasion. In charge of Transport he would wake up whole battalions and rush them to various points of the harbour or coastline, absolutely certain that the Japanese would not come by plane but by ship. Marble Beach, Coral Beach, Nilaveli, Elephant Point, Frenchman's Pass, all suddenly began to glow like fireflies from army jeeps sent there at three in the morning. He began to drink a lot, moved onto a plateau of constant alcohol, and had to be hospitalized. Authorities decided to send him back to a military hospital in Colombo under the care of John Kotelawela, once more the unfortunate travelling companion. (Sir John Kotelawela, for he was eventually to become Prime Minister.) Somehow my father smuggled bottles of gin onto the train and even before they left Trinco he was raging. The train sped through tunnels, scrubland, careened around sharp bends, and my father's fury imitated it, its speed and shake and loudness, he blew in and out of carriages, heaving bottles out of the windows as he finished them, getting John Kotelawela's gun.

More drama was taking place off the train as his relatives tried to intercept it before he reached Colombo. For some reason it was crucial that he be taken to hospital by a member of the family rather than under military guard. His sister, my Aunt Stephy, drove to meet the train at Anuradhapura, not quite sure what his condition was but sure that she was his favourite sister. Unfortunately she arrived at the station in a white silk dress, a white feathered hat, and a long white pair of gloves — perhaps to impress John Kotelawela who was in charge of her brother and who was attracted to her. Her looks gathered such a crowd and caused such an uproar that she was surrounded and couldn't reach the carriage when the train slowed into the station. John Kotelawela glanced at her with wonder — this slight, demure, beautiful woman in white on the urine-soaked platform — while he struggled with her brother who had begun to take off his clothes.

"Mervyn!"

"Stephy!"

Shouted as they passed each other, the train pulling out, Stephy still being mobbed, and an empty bottle crashing onto the end of the platform like a last sentence.

John Kotelawela was knocked out by my father before he reached Galgamuwa. He never pressed charges. In any case my father took over the train.

He made it shunt back and forth ten miles one way, ten miles another, so that all trains, some full of troops, were grounded in the south unable to go anywhere. He managed to get the driver of the train drunk as well and was finishing a bottle of gin every hour walking up and down the carriages almost naked, but keeping his shoes on this time and hitting the state of inebriation during which he would start rattling off wonderful limericks — thus keeping the passengers amused.

But there was another problem to contend with. One whole carriage was given over to high-ranking British officers. They had retired early and, while the train witnessed small revolutions among the local military, everyone felt that the anarchic events should be kept from the sleeping foreigners. The English thought Ceylon trains were bad enough, and if they discovered that officers in the Ceylon Light Infantry were going berserk and upsetting schedules they might just leave the country in disgust. Therefore, if anyone wished to reach the other end of the train, they would climb onto the roof of the "English carriage" and tiptoe, silhouetted by the moon above them, to the next compartment. My father, too, whenever he needed to speak with the driver, climbed out into the night and strolled over the train, clutching a bottle and revolver and greeting passengers in hushed tones who were coming the other way. Fellow officers who were trying to subdue him would never have considered waking up the English. They slept on serenely with their rage for order in the tropics, while the train shunted and reversed into the night and there was chaos and hilarity in the parentheses around them.

Meanwhile, my Uncle Noel, fearful that my father would be charged, was waiting for the train at Kelaniya six miles out of Colombo, quite near where my father had stopped the train to wait for Arthur van Langenberg. So they knew him well there. But the train kept shunting back and forth, never reaching Kelaniya, because at this point my father was absolutely certain the Japanese had mined the train with bombs, which would explode if they reached Colombo. Therefore, anyone who was without a military connection was put off the train at Polgahawela, and he cruised up and down the carriages breaking all the lights that would heat the bombs. He was saving the train and Colombo. While my Uncle Noel waited for over six hours at Kelaniya — the train coming into sight and then retreating once more to the north — my father and two officers under his control searched every piece of luggage. He alone found over twenty-five bombs and as he collected them the others became silent and no longer argued. There were now only fifteen people, save for the sleeping English, on the Trinco-Colombo train, which eventually, as night was ending and the gin ran out, drifted into Kelaniya. My father and the driver had consumed almost seven bottles since that morning.

My Uncle Noel put the bruised John Kotelawela in the back of the Navy jeep he had borrowed. And then my father said he couldn't leave the bombs on the train, they had to take them in the jeep and drop them into the river. He rushed back time and again into the train and brought out the pots of curd that passengers had been carrying. They were carefully loaded into the jeep alongside the prone body of the future Prime Minister. Before my Uncle drove to the hospital, he stopped at the Kelani-Colombo bridge and my father dropped all twenty-five pots into the river below, witnessing huge explosions as they smashed into the water.

SIR JOHN

Gillian and I drive south on the Galle Road, and just past Ratmalana Airport turn inland to the home of Sir John Kotelawela. The jeep dusty, covered in 3-in-1 Oil, moves through the long palatial driveway of red earth and into sudden greenery. A small man in white shirt and shorts, very thin legs, sits on the porch waiting for us. As we park he gets up slowly. We have been invited for breakfast with Sir John and it is 8:30 in the morning.

I have spoken to him on the phone but he seems to have forgotten why we are here, though he is expecting us at breakfast. Gillian and I give our names once more. Mervyn Ondaatje's children. You knew him in the Ceylon Light Infantry?

"Ahh!"

His diplomat's face is utterly shocked. "That one!" he says. "The fellow who got us into all that trouble!" and begins laughing. The last people in the world this millionaire and ex-Prime

Minister probably expected to see were the children of Mervyn Ondaatje — the officer who got the D.T.'s in Trincomalee and took a notorious train ride to Colombo in 1943. This is probably the first time anyone has come not so much to see him, *the* Sir John Kotelawela, but because he happened to know for a few hectic months during the war a consistently drunk officer in the Ceylon Light Infantry.

After about ten minutes he still isn't over this bizarre motive for the visit. A servant brings him a cane basket full of fruit, and bread, and scones. Sir John says "come" and begins to stroll into the garden with the food under his arm. I gather we are to have breakfast under the trees. As we usually eat at seven in the morning, Gillian and I are both starving. He walks slowly towards a series of aquariums on the other side of the pool and driveway. "My fish from Australia," he says, and begins to feed them from the basket. I lift my head to see a peacock on the roof spreading his tail.

"Hell of a lot of trouble that one caused." What? "You know he jumped out of the train when it was going full speed . . . luckily we were passing a paddy field and he fell into it. When the train stopped he just climbed aboard again covered with mud." It is a Victorian dream. We are on the lawn, my sister Gillian, this frail and powerful man, and we are surrounded by four or five peacocks who are consuming my scones, leaning in jerks towards the basket he holds. And interspersed among the peacocks as if imitating them are sprinklers which throw off tails of white, keeping the birds company. Now it is time to feed the sambhur deer and jungle fowl.

In the next half hour we ease him back into the story three times and, his memory finally alive to the forties, he remembers more and more. All through his narrative he never calls my father by his name, christian or surname, just "this chap," or "that fellow." He is enjoying the story now. I've heard it from three or four other points of view and can remind him of certain bones — the pots of curd, etc.

"I was the commanding officer, you see. He had been drinking for months. Then one night at two in the morning he drives into the base in his jeep. He says the Japanese have invaded. He's found one. Well I didn't think so, but I climbed into the jeep and drove off with him. There was a man five yards out in the surf standing there like a statue. This fellow says, "There he is." He had found him two hours earlier coming ashore, halted him, fired his pistol into the water between the man's legs and said, stay there, stay right there, *do not move* till I get back, and jumped into the jeep and came to get us at the base. I put the jeep lights on him and we could see right away he was a Tamil. So then I knew.

"Next morning I took him with me to Colombo by train. He played hell on the way."

The sambhur has eaten all the bananas, so we go back in, join Sir John's doctor and the doctor's wife and sit down in an open dining room to the real breakfast.

Sir John's breakfasts are legendary, always hoppers and fish curry, mangoes and curd. A breeze blows magically under the table, a precise luxury, and I stretch my feet to its source as I tear apart the first hopper. My sandal is wrenched off and goes flying down under the length of the table, luckily not in the direction of Sir John. My foot tingling. While everyone else eats I lean back and look underneath and there is a small portable fan a few inches from my toes ready to tear into flesh this time. I could have lost a toe during one of these breakfasts searching for my father.

Sir John is talking about someone else now, delighting in some scandal about "one of the best liars we have." The open windows that come down to within six inches of the floor have no glass. A crow steps up as if to make an announcement, moves away and then the peacock climbs in and steps down to the light brown parquet floor. His feet give a slight click at each step. No one has seen this wonder, it seems, but me. Sir John reaches for a hopper, tears off the brittle edges of the dough, and taking the soft delicious centre, holds it out and the peacock he has not even looked at but hears, perhaps just senses, takes a final step forward, declines his neck and accepts the hopper walking away to a less busy part of the dining room, eating as he walks.

While we eat, an amateur theatre group from Colombo which is producing *Camelot* receives permission to be photographed on the grounds. The dream-like setting is now made more surreal by Sinhalese actors wearing thick velvet costumes, pointed hats, and chain mail in this terrible May heat. A group of black knights mime festive songs among the peacocks and fountains. Guinevere kisses Arthur beside the tank of Australian fish.

The photographers outside, the idea of *Camelot*, all remind Sir John of his political tribulations. For he claims that if anything lost him elections it was the grandness of the house and his parties — pictures of which appeared in the newspapers. He tells us of one of the most scandalous photographs organized by the Opposition. A demure young couple visited him along with a third friend who had a camera. They asked if he minded their taking some photographs and he gave them permission. The photographer took several pictures of the couple. Suddenly the man dropped to his knees, lifted up the woman's sari and started chewing away at her upper thigh. Sir John who was watching casually a few yards away rushed forward and asked what was happening. The man on his knees unburied his head and grinned at him saying, "snake bite, sir," and returned to the thigh of the woman.

A week later three photographs appeared in the newspapers of this blatantly sexual act with Sir John also in the picture chatting casually to the woman whose face was in the throes of ecstasy.

PHOTOGRAPH

My Aunt pulls out the album and there is the photograph I have been waiting for all my life. My father and mother together. May 1932.

They are on their honeymoon and the two of them, very soberly dressed, have walked into a photographic studio. The photographer is used to wedding pictures. He has probably seen every pose. My father sits facing the camera, my mother stands beside him and bends over so that her face is in profile on a level with his. Then they both begin to make hideous faces.

My father's pupils droop to the south-west corner of his sockets. His jaw falls and resettles into a groan that is half idiot, half shock. (All this emphasized by his dark suit and well-combed hair.) My mother in white has twisted her lovely features and stuck out her jaw and upper lip so that her profile is in the posture of a monkey. The print is made into a postcard and sent through

143

the mails to various friends. On the back my father has written *"What we think of married life."*

Everything is there, of course. Their good looks behind the tortured faces, their mutual humour, and the fact that both of them are hams of a very superior sort. The evidence I wanted that they were absolutely perfect for each other. My father's tanned skin, my mother's milk paleness, and this theatre of their own making.

It is the only photograph I have found of the two of them together.

WHAT WE THINK
OF MARRIED LIFE

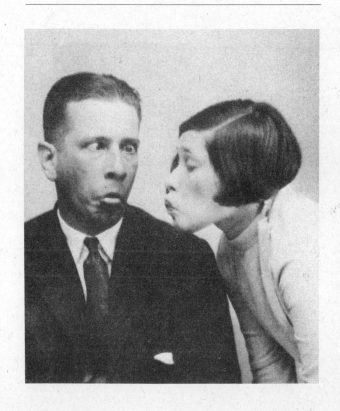

TEA COUNTRY

"The thing about Mum was — she was a terrifically social person. And he came down to Colombo and swooped her up and took her to the tea estate. OK. They were in love, happy with each other, they had kids. But later there was nothing for her to do there."

Tea country. The sleepy green landscape that held her captive. And now, 40 years later, in early May, on the verge of monsoon weather, I have come here to visit my half-sister Susan and her husband Sunil. The green pattern of landscape and life-style almost unchanged.

The one hundred mile drive from Colombo took us five hours. The gearshift was giving trouble, the horn was fading, and the engine heated up so fast we had to stop every twenty minutes to cool off and refill the radiator. We came along a road that climbed five thousand feet in thirty miles. Eventually the transmission broke in second gear, and the last miles were driven praying we wouldn't have to stop, not for oncoming trucks and buses, not for the numerous May Day parades along the mountain roads. The car stalled a mile away from the house and we walked under the thunder clouds that made the dark tea bushes brighter, through the lines of pluckers, Sunil carrying his Colombo whiskey and Susan and I some bags of food.

In a wet shirt and with a headache it was good to walk. Twenty degrees cooler up here than in Colombo. And a sourceless light that seems to brighten the landscape from underneath, as if yellow flowers in the garden are leaking into wet air. Dampness hangs over the house, while three of us and one servant rattle around this huge long bungalow from which all furniture has been sent to be upholstered save for a few cane chairs, and where the loudest noise is the excited breathing of two dogs.

An hour later I am standing in the hall with Susan when I hear a pistol shot. Blue waves of flame. The house — hit by lightning, hit at the fuse-box on the wall just above my head. I am so shaken I act calmly for the rest of the afternoon. Lightning has never touched this house before even though, perched on top of a tea estate, it seems an obvious target. The bolt is a signal for the end of quietness and the weather bursts open windows and steps into hallways. During the long evening we play scrabble, shouting out scores, almost unable to be heard over the stereophonic field of the rain.

*   *   *

We wake to a silence. Now the long quiet mornings. Susan moves up and down halls to the kitchens, organizing meals, reorganizing after the chaos of the first monsoon storm (burned out fuse-boxes, knocked down telephone wires, chicken wires, dismantled gardens).

The dining room doors open to the wet lawn and the francisco bushes. Their blossoms, like torn blue and white paper, release perfume into this room. When the dogs bark, eight or so parakeets swerve out of the guava tree and disappear over the cliff of the hill. Across the valley, a waterfall stumbles down. In a month or two the really hard rains will come for eighteen hours a day and that waterfall will once again become tough as a glacier and wash away the road. But now it looks as delicate as the path of a white butterfly in a long-exposed photograph.

I can leave this table, walk ten yards out of the house, and be surrounded by versions of green. The most regal green being the tea bush which is regal also in its symmetrical efficient planting. Such precision would be jungle in five years if left alone. In the distance the tea pickers move, in another silence, like an army. The roads weave and whorl away — bright yellow under the grey sky. The sun, invisible, struggles up somewhere. This is the colour of landscape, this is the silence, that surrounded my parents' marriage.

"WHAT WE THINK OF
MARRIED LIFE"

She is very gentle, Susan, my half-sister. Almost utterly humble. So sitting here with Susan and Sunil I find myself surprised they are younger than me. She has this calmness and quietness as opposed to the anger and argument which I see in myself, my brother, and two sisters.

I have been thinking that if she has Ondaatje blood and no Gratiaen blood then obviously it is from my mother's side that we got a sense of the dramatic, the tall stories, the determination to now and then hold the floor. The ham in us. While from my father, in spite of his temporary manic public behaviour, we got our sense of secrecy, the desire to be reclusive.

My father loved books and so did my mother, but my father swallowed the heart of books and kept that knowledge and emotion to himself. My mother read her favourite poems out loud, would make us read plays together and acted herself, even running a small dance and theatre school that people still remember in Colombo. Her reading out loud demanded the whole room, and while young her grace and dancing caught everyone's attention. Later it was her voice, her stories with that husky wheezing laugh that almost drowned out the punch lines. She belonged to a type of Ceylonese family whose women would take the minutest reaction from another and blow it up into a tremendously exciting tale, then later use it as an example of someone's strain of character. If anything kept their generation alive it was this recording by exaggeration. Ordinary tennis matches would be mythologized to the extent that one player was so drunk that he almost died on the court. An individual would be eternally remembered for one small act that in five years had become so magnified he was just a footnote below it. The silence of the tea estates and no doubt my mother's sense of theatre and romance (fed by vociferous readings of J. M. Barrie and Michael Arlen) combined the edited delicacies of fiction with the last era of a colonial Ceylon.

My father's actions were minimal and more private. Although he tormented his own father's rules of decorum he simultaneously and almost secretly valued the elements of honour and gentleness. He reportedly couldn't stand his mother-in-law, Lalla, for what he saw as her crudeness, although the stories about my father are closer in style to those about Lalla than anyone else. While we used to love rushing around the house and estate at Lalla's insistence to catch the dog Chindit, who had run off with her false breast, my father would retire to a book or his office acutely embarrassed. Either that, or, and of this we were never sure, he would secretly train the dog to torment his mother-in-law by such acts. We know he encouraged Chindit to fart whenever possible in her vicinity and by raising his eyebrows would surreptitiously make us feel it was she who made us recoil to the other end of the room.

My father's dramatic nature pleased only himself and sometimes the four of us. Or he would tell a hilarious joke in everyone's presence that would convulse just my mother and himself.

My mother loved, *always* loved, even in her last years long after their divorce, his secretive and slightly crooked humour. It bound them together probably more than anything. They were in a world to themselves, genial with everyone but sharing a code of humour. And if there was to be drama in their lives my father preferred it to be just between the two of them. My mother on the other hand would somehow select the one action that would be remembered by everyone in the vicinity of the tea estate and would reach Colombo in twenty-four hours. On one of the last occasions that my mother left my father, after the tirade that was brief, loud, alcoholically one-sided, she told him she was leaving him at 11:00 P.M. She bundled us all up and, after my father grabbed the car key and threw it into the darkness of a hundred tea bushes, she got four servants and with each of us on a pair of shoulders, marched off through tea estate and dense jungle in utter darkness to a neighbouring home five miles away.

It was she who instilled theatre in all of us. She was determined that we would each be as good an actor as she was. Whenever my father would lapse into one of his alcoholic states, she would send the three older children (I would be asleep — too young, and oblivious) into my father's room where by now he could hardly talk let alone argue. The three of them, well coached, would perform with tears streaming, "Daddy, don't drink, daddy, if you love us, don't drink," while my mother waited outside and listened. My father, I hope, too far gone to know the extent of the wars against him. These moments embarrassed my older brother and sister terribly; for days after they felt guilty and miserable. Gillian, the youngest of the three, threw herself with eagerness into these one-act plays and when they returned to the living room my mother would pat her on the back and say, "Well done Gillian — you were by *far* the best."

Her motive was to cure my father of manic alcoholic consumption. Those were moments of total war as far as she was concerned. During all the months of soberness the two of them were equals, very close and full of humour, but in his moments of darkness she drew on every play she had been in or had read and used it as a weapon, knowing that when my father sobered up this essentially shy man would be appalled to hear how my mother had over-reacted. Her behaviour in his drunken moments was there to shock him in his times of gentleness when he loved muted behaviour. Whatever plays my mother acted in publicly were not a patch on the real-life drama she directed and starred in during her married life. If Mervyn was to humiliate her she could embarrass him by retaliating with some grand gesture — whether it was a celebrated walk through the jungle or actually holding her breath until she fainted at the Kitulgala resthouse when she saw him beginning to drink too much, so that he had to stop and drive her home.

His victories came when he was sober. Then he would discover some outrageous thing she had done and begin to mend fences. Within a week, by his charm and wit, he would have made my mother's behaviour more ludicrous than his — a bomb to disturb a butterfly, till he seemed the more sane of the two. In this way an incident, which most had felt could never be surmounted and which no doubt would destroy the marriage, was cemented over. Rather than being jealous, my mother was never happier and for the next six months or so they were delightful company, wonderful parents. And then with the first drink, after which he could almost never stop, the wars would begin again.

Finally, when it all came to an end, she played her last scene with him. She arrived at the divorce court in a stunning white dress and hat (she had never worn a hat in her life before) and calmly asked for a divorce, demanding no alimony — nothing for her and nothing for the children. She got a job at the Grand Oriental Hotel, trained herself as a housekeeper-manager and supported us through schools by working in hotels in Ceylon and then England till she died. The easy life of the tea estate and the theatrical wars were over. They had come a long way in fourteen years from being the products of two of the best known and wealthiest families in Ceylon: my father now owning only a chicken farm at Rock Hill, my mother working in a hotel.

Before my mother left for England in 1949 she went to a fortune-teller who predicted that while she would continue to see each of her children often for the rest of her life, she would never see them all together again. This turned out to be true. Gillian stayed in Ceylon with me, Christopher and Janet went to England. I went to England, Christopher went to Canada, Gillian came to England, Janet went to America, Gillian returned to Ceylon, Janet returned to England, I went to Canada. Magnetic fields would go crazy in the presence of more than three Ondaatjes. And my father. Always separate until he died, away from us. The north pole.

DIALOGUES

(i)

"Once he nearly killed us. Not you. But the three older children. He was driving the Ford and he was drunk and taking the corners with great swerves — and you know those up-country roads. We began by cheering but soon we were terrified. Yelling at him to stop. Finally on one corner he almost went off the cliff. Two wheels had gone over the edge and the car hung there caught on the axle. Below us was a terrific plunge down the mountainside. We were in the back seat and once we calmed down, we looked in the front seat and saw that Daddy was asleep. He had passed out. But to us he was asleep and that seemed much worse. *Much* too casual.

As he had been driving he was on the right hand side — the side which was about to tilt over, so we all scrambled to the left. But if we climbed into the front seat and got out then he would have gone over by himself. We didn't know what to do. We had passed some tea pluckers a few hundred yards back and the only hope was that they might be able to lift the car back onto the road. We decided the lightest one should go but Janet and Gillian got into a fight as to who was the lightest. They were both sensitive about their weight at the time. Finally Gillian went off and Janet and I tried to pull him towards the passenger seat.

When he wakened the car had already been lifted and moved to the centre of the road. He felt better, he said, started the car up and told us to hop in. But none of us would get into the car again."

(ii)

"I remember when Daddy lost his job. He had just been sacked and he was drinking. Mummy was in the front seat with him, you and I were in the back. And for the whole trip he kept saying 'I'm ruined. I've ruined all of you. All of you.' And he would weep. It was a terrible trip. And Mum kept comforting him and saying she would never leave him, she would never leave him. Do you remember that . . .?"

(iii)

"When I left for England, god that was a terrible day for Mum. We were all at Kuttapitiya and she drove me down to Colombo. Left early in the morning. She had to move fast. He was drinking such a lot then and she couldn't leave him for too long. So when we boarded the ship, *The Queen of Bermuda*, that was about the time he was waking up and she had to get back before he got into trouble. She knew he had already begun his drinking as she said goodbye to me."

(iv)

"Remember all the pillows he had to sleep with? Remember how he used to make us massage his legs? Each of us had to do it for ten minutes. . . ."

(v)

"To us he was an utterly charming man, always gracious. When you spoke to him you knew you were speaking to the *real* Mervyn. He was always so open and loved those he visited. But none of us knew what he was like when he was drunk. So when your mother spoke of the reasons for the break-up it was a complete surprise. Oh I did see him drunk once and he was a bloody nuisance, but only once.

Anyway she told us things were rough. Their servant, Gopal, would not obey her and would continue to buy your father bottles. So we suggested the two of them go up to 'Ferncliff' in Nuwara Eliya. They stayed there a week but that didn't work out and they returned to Kegalle. He had lost his job by then, so they were at home most of the time. Then your mother got typhoid. Para-typhoid, not the most serious kind, but she had it — and he wouldn't believe her. She said he hit her to make her get out of bed. Somehow she convinced Gopal how serious it was, and while he always obeyed your father he went into town and phoned us. We drove her down to Colombo and put her in Spittel's Nursing Home.

She never went back to him. When she was released she went and lived with Noel and Zillah at Horton Place.

Anyway, a few years later we decided to work on the lawn at 'Ferncliff' which was turning brown. So we arranged to have some turf delivered from the Golf Club. And when we started digging we found about thirty bottles of Rocklands Gin buried in that front lawn by your father. . . ."

(vi)

"I don't know when this happened or how old I was. I was lying on a bed. It was night. The room was being thrown around and they were shouting. Like giants."

(vii)

"After leaving him she worked at the Mount Lavinia Hotel and then the Grand Oriental Hotel, that's called the Taprobane now. Then in the fifties she moved to England. She had a rough time during those early years in England, working at that boarding house in Lancaster Gate. She had one small room with just a gas ring. Noel's daughter, Wendy, was boarded at a private school at the time and she was wonderful. Every weekend she'd tell all her Cheltenham friends "Now we must go and visit Aunt Doris," and she'd drag these posh English school girls, about 6 or 7 of them, and they'd crowd into that small bed-sitter and cook crumpets over the gas ring."

(viii)

"I had some friends who played tennis. My best friends in London. And they were invited to Ceylon for a tournament. They were there for two weeks. When they came back to England I didn't contact them. Never answered their calls. You see I thought they would have found out what a disgraceful family I had come from. Mummy had drummed this story into us about what we had all been through there. I had this image that the Ondaatjes were absolute pariahs. I was twenty-five years old then. When I went back five years later to Ceylon to see Gillian I was still nervous and was totally surprised that everyone remembered him and all of us with such delight and love. . . ."

(ix)

"In the end he used to come to Colombo every two weeks to bring me eggs and fertilizer for my garden. He was subdued then, no longer the irrepressible Mervyn we used to know, very kind and quiet. He was happy just to sit here and listen to me gab away. . . . I never met his second wife, Maureen, until the day of his funeral."

(x)

"You know what I remember best is how sad his face was. I would be doing something and suddenly look up and catch his face naked. And full of sorrow. I don't know. Long after the divorce I wrote to him. I'd just been to my first dance and I complained about all the soppy songs the boys sang to us, especially one they played constantly, which went "Kiss me once and kiss me twice and kiss me once again . . . it's been a *long long* time," and he wrote back saying he just wished he could kiss us all once again. . . . The sections you sent me made me very sad, remembering him and all those times. Of course I was always the serious one among us, with no sense of humour. I showed what you had written to someone and they laughed and said what a wonderful childhood we must have had, and I said it was a nightmare."

(xi)

"When I used to meet him years later he was always a fund of wonderful stories, never dirty, never mocked a woman. Anyway, one day I ran into him in the Fort and that night your mother, who was visiting Ceylon at the time, came to dinner. So, playing the devil's advocate, I told her who I had seen that morning and I said, *you* should see him. I remember she was very silent and looked down at her empty plate and around the room, somewhat surprised, and said, 'Why should I have to see him?' And I don't know why but I kept pushing it and then gradually she began to be interested. I think she almost gave in. I said I could easily reach him by phone, he could come over and join us. They were both in their sixties then, hadn't seen each other even once since the divorce. For old time's sake, Doris, I said, just to see each other. Then my wife thought I was being too cocky and made me change the subject and suggested we eat, that dinner was ready. But I know she was nearly persuaded to, I could tell that more than anything else. It was so close. . . ."

BLIND FAITH

During certain hours, at certain years in our lives, we see ourselves as remnants from the earlier generations that were destroyed. So our job becomes to keep peace with enemy camps, eliminate the chaos at the end of Jacobean tragedies, and with "the mercy of distance" write the histories.

Fortinbras. Edgar. Christopher, my sisters, Wendy, myself. I think all of our lives have been terribly shaped by what went on before us. And why of Shakespeare's cast of characters do I remain most curious about Edgar? Who if I look deeper into the metaphor, torments his father over an imaginary cliff.

Words such as *love*, *passion*, *duty*, are so continually used they grow to have no meaning — except as coins or weapons. Hard language softens. I never knew what my father felt of these "things." My loss was that I never spoke to him as an adult. Was he locked in the ceremony of being "a father"? He died before I even thought of such things.

I long for the moment in the play where Edgar reveals himself to Gloucester and it never happens. Look I am the son who has grown up. I am the son you have made hazardous, who still loves you. I am now part of an adult's ceremony, but I want to say I am writing this book about you at a time when I am least sure about such words. . . . Give me your arm. Let go my hand. Give me your arm. Give the word. "Sweet Marjoram" . . . a tender herb.

THE BONE

There is a story about my father I cannot come to terms with. It is one of the versions of his train escapade. In this one he had escaped from the train and run off naked into the jungle. ("Your father had a runaway complex," someone has already told me.) His friend Arthur was called to find him and persuade him back. When Arthur eventually tracked him down this is what he saw.

My father is walking towards him, huge and naked. In one hand he holds five ropes, and dangling on the end of each of them is a black dog. None of the five are touching the ground. He is holding his arm outstretched, holding them with one arm as if he has supernatural strength. Terrible noises are coming from him and from the dogs as if there is a conversation between them that is subterranean, volcanic. All their tongues hanging out.

They were probably stray dogs which my father had stumbled on in jungle villages, he had perhaps picked them up as he walked along. He was a man who loved dogs. But this scene had no humour or gentleness in it. The dogs were too powerful to be in danger of being strangled. The danger was to the naked man who held them at arm's length, towards whom they swung like large dark magnets. He did not recognize Arthur, he would not let go of the ropes. He had captured all the evil in the regions he had passed through and was holding it.

Arthur cut the ropes and the animals splashed to the ground, writhing free and escaping. He guided my father back to the road and the car that his sister Stephy waited in. They put him in the back seat, his arm still held away from him, now out of the open car window. All the way to Colombo the lengths of rope dangled from his fist in the hot passing air.

THE CEYLON CACTUS
AND SUCCULENT SOCIETY

"THANIKAMA"

After the morning's drive to Colombo, after the meeting with Doris — tense, speaking in whispers in the hotel lobby — he would force himself to sit on the terrace overlooking the sea. Would sit in the sunlight drinking beers, which he ordered ice-cold, and finishing them before the sweat even evaporated from the surface of the bottle. Poured out the glasses of Nuwara Eliya beer. He sat there all afternoon, hoping she would notice him and come down to speak with him properly, truthfully. He wanted his wife to stop this *posing* at her work. Had to speak with her. He could hardly remember where the children were now. Two in school in England, one in Kegalle, one in Colombo. . . .

Till 5 o'clock, he sat out on the blue terrace with the blaze of sun on him — determined to be somewhere where they could be alone if she changed her mind and came down to him — not with the other guests and drinkers in the cool shadows of the lobby of the Mount Lavinia Hotel. He recalled everyone. Their crowd. Noel, Trevor, Francis who was dead now, Dorothy who ran riot. All burghers and Sinhalese families, separate from the Europeans. The memory of his friends was with him in the sun. He poured them out of the bottles into his glass tankard and drank. He remembered Harold Tooby from his schooldays and his years at Cambridge where the code was "you can always get away with more than you think you can get away with. . . ." Till Lionel Wendt accidentally told his father of the deception. Lionel always guilty over this, who gave him and Doris a painting by George Keyt for their wedding. He still had that in any case, and the wooden statue of a woman he had picked up at an auction which everyone else hated. Objects had stayed and people disappeared.

At five he got into the white Ford. She had not come down to him. And he drove to F. X. Pereira in the Ridgeway Building and bought cases of beer and gin to take back to Kegalle. Then he parked near the Galle Face Hotel, old haunt, and crossed the street to the bar where journalists and others from Lake House sat and talked politics, talked rubbish, talked about sport, which he was not at all interested in now. Did not mention Doris. Drank and laughed and listened, till eleven at night at which time they all went home to their wives. He walked down Galle Road and ate a meal at a Muslim restaurant, sitting alone in one of the frail wooden booths, the food so hot it would sear back the drunkenness and sleepiness, and then got into his car. This was 1947.

He drove along Galle Face Green where the Japanese had eventually attacked, by plane, and disappeared into the Fort whose streets were dark and quiet and empty. He loved the Fort at this hour, these Colombo nights, the windows of his car open and the breeze for the first time almost cool, no longer tepid, hitting his face with all the night smells, the perfume of closed boutiques.

An animal crossed the road and he braked to a halt and watched it, strolling at its own speed for it was midnight and if a car would actually stop it could be trusted. This animal paused when it reached the pavement and looked back at the man in the white car — who still had not moved on. They gazed at each other and then the creature ran up the steps of the white building and into the post office which stayed open all night.

He thought, I could sleep here too. I could leave the car in the centre of Queen's Road and go in. Other cars would weave around the Ford. It would disturb no one for four or five hours. Nothing would change. He lifted his foot off the clutch, pressed the accelerator and moved on through the Fort towards Mutwal, passed the church of his ancestors — all priests and doctors and translators — which looked down on him through a row of plantain trees, looked down onto the ships in the harbour docked like enormous sinking jewels. He drove out of Colombo.

An hour later he could have stopped at the Ambepussa rest-house but continued on, the day's alcohol still in him though he had already stopped twice on the side of the road, urinated into darkness and mysterious foliage. Halted briefly at Warakapola where the dark villages held the future and gave a Tamil a lift, the man striking up a conversation about stars, and he, proud of that mutual ancestry, discussing Orion with him. The man was a cinnamon peeler and the smell filled the car, he did not want to stop, wanted to take him all the way past the spice gardens to Kegalle rather than letting him out a mile up the road. He drove on, the cinnamon blown out already by new smells from the night, drove dangerously, he couldn't quite remember if he was driving dangerously or not, just aware of the night breezes, the fall-out from spice gardens he skirted as if driving past vast kitchens. One of the lamps of his car was dead so he knew he was approaching stray walkers disguised as a motorcycle. He weaved up the Nelundeniya U-turns, then into the town of Kegalle. Over the bridge into Rock Hill.

For about ten minutes he sat in front of the house now fully aware that the car was empty but for his body, this corpse. Leaving the car door open like a white broken wing on the lawn, he moved towards the porch, a case of liquor under his arm. *Moonless.* The absence of even an edge of the moon. Into the bedroom, the bottle top already unscrewed. Tooby, Tooby, you should see your school friend now. The bottle top in my mouth as I sit on the bed like a lost ship on a white sea. And they sat years ago on deck-chairs, young, going to England. In the absurd English clothes they surprised each other with. And then during the heart of the marriage sailed to Australia serene over the dark mountains in the sea, the bed of the ocean like a dragon's back, ridges and troughs and the darkest eye of the Diamantina crater. This too was part of the universe, a feature of the earth. Kissed in the botanical gardens of Perth, took the Overland train east across the country just so they could say they had seen the Pacific. His Colombo suit fell off him now to the floor, onto its own pool of white and he got into bed. Thinking. What was he thinking about? More and more he watched himself do nothing, with nothing. At moments like this.

He saw himself with the bottle. Where was his book. He had lost it. What was the book. It was not Shakespeare, not those plays of love he wept over too easily. With dark blue bindings. You creaked them open and stepped into a roomful of sorrow. A mid-summer dream. All of them had moved at times with an ass's head, Titania Dorothy Hilden Lysander de Saram, a mongrel collection part Sinhalese part Dutch part Tamil part ass moving slowly in the forests with foolish and serious obsessions. No, he looked around the bare room, don't talk to me about Shakespeare, about "green hats."

The bottle was half empty beside him. He arose and lit the kerosene lamp. He wanted to look at his face, though the mirror was stained as if brown water and rust hung captive in the glass. He stepped towards the bathroom, the yellow pendulum of lamp beside his knees. With each swing he witnessed the state of the room and corridor. A glimpse of cobwebs quickly aging, undusted glass. No sweeper for weeks. And nature advanced. Tea bush became jungle, branches put their arms into the windows. If you stood still you were invaded. Wealth that was static quickly rotted. The paper money in your pocket, wet from your own sweat, gathered mould.

In the bathroom ants had attacked the novel thrown on the floor by the commode. A whole battalion was carrying one page away from its source, carrying the intimate print as if rolling a tablet away from him. He knelt down on the red tile, slowly, not wishing to disturb their work. It was page *171*. He had not got that far in the book yet but he surrendered it to them. He sat down forgetting the mirror he had been moving towards. Scared of the company of the mirror. He sat down with his back against the wall and waited. The white rectangle moved with the busy arduous ants. Duty, he thought. But that was just a fragment gazed at by the bottom of his eye. He drank. There. He saw the midnight rat.

MONSOON NOTEBOOK (iii)

A school exercise book. I write this at the desk of calamander looking out of the windows into dry black night. "Thanikama." "Aloneness." Birdless. The sound of an animal passing through the garden. Midnight and noon and dawn and dusk are the hours of danger, susceptibility to the "grahayas"— planetary spirits of malignant character. Avoid eating certain foods in lonely places, the devils will smell you out. Carry some metal. An iron heart. Do not step on bone or hair or human ash.

Sweat down my back. The fan pauses then begins again. At midnight this hand is the only thing moving. As discreetly and carefully as whatever animals in the garden fold brown leaves into their mouths, visit the drain for water, or scale the broken glass that crowns the walls. Watch the hand move. Waiting for it to say something, to stumble casually on perception, the shape of an unknown thing.

The garden a few feet away is suddenly under the fist of a downpour. Within half a second an easy dry night is filled with the noise of rain on tin, cement and earth — waking others slowly in the house. But I actually saw it, looking out into the blackness, saw the white downpour (reflected off the room's light) falling like an object past the window. And now the dust that has been there for months is bounced off the earth and pours, the smell of it, into the room. I get up, walk to the night, and breathe it in — the dust, the tactile smell of wetness, oxygen now being pounded into the ground so it is difficult to breathe.

FINAL DAYS
FATHER TONGUE

Jennifer:

The poultry farm was very big then. He had thousands of chickens. He had dual-purpose breeds — those that laid eggs but could also be eaten. The Light Sussex, the Rhode Island Reds, the Plymouth Rocks. And he was also the Visiting Agent for the region, inspecting estates and writing up reports on how they were run . . . I think he was one of the first Ceylonese to become a V.A. But the chickens took up most of his time. I designed a poster for the poultry farm and he got them printed up grandly. And we would dream up these advertisements together for the newspapers. Many were not allowed by the *Daily News* such as "Rock Hill Farms Will Teach your Grandmother to Suck Eggs!" He kept us all busy. I did the correspondence and Susan collected the eggs. It would have been easy to be cut off at Kegalle but he built a world for us there — all those books and radio programmes. We would listen to "20 Questions" — my god we heard that every week and he loved it and I hated it.

During the day he would invent jobs for which he would pay us. Now and then he would announce "Beetle Week." We had to catch black coconut beetles, which he then fed to his fowls. Ten cents for the large ones, five cents for the small ones, and we would spend hours sorting them out and deciding if they were large or small. The whole day would be organized like this, with these games. For instance, *cats*. He loved most animals but was aloof from cats. However they always followed him. So if he went into town we would take bets on how many cats would come up to him. And although he disliked them I think he was quite proud of this trait in himself. Cats would cross the street if they saw him coming. When we got into the car he would have to get in first and we would then have to start throwing them out, have to stop them crawling back under his seat.

He loved our gullibility, our innocence, and his tricks on us would last for years. When he picked Suzie and me up from boarding school for a day he would take us to Elephant House and order cakes and cream buns and Lanka Colas. He had at one time said, "the more you eat the less I'll have to pay," and we believed him and for *his* sake ate as much as we could. It was only when Maureen came with him once and was appalled by our greed that we discovered the truth and we were almost slapped for our stupidity.

He could make children behave because he kept them interested. You, apparently, were a saint when Daddy was around but if he left the house you were hell. He missed you all terribly, he longed for you, but with us — his second family — he was just as loving.

I wasn't his real daughter but I was probably closest to him in his last years. He brought me up like a princess and would defend me against everyone, even my strictest teachers. There was a Miss Kaula — a battleaxe. She was charmed by Daddy. She preened herself before he arrived and allowed him to upset all the visiting hours. He was amazingly protective. He would never let me stay with friends over the weekend, they would have to come and stay with us. And if there wasn't enough food to go around he would announce these signals such as "F.H.B.", which meant "Family Hold Back." We loved all those codes. The only time I saw him totally lost was when I begged him to take me to a movie. It was a "twist" movie. Joey D. and the Starlighters in *Peppermint Twist*. He was horrified by it. It was the future.

He could always laugh at himself. He was so big in the end, so large. He donated 313 rupees to the Rotary Club and when he was asked why it was that amount, he said because that was his weight. I think it was a glandular problem but he just didn't bother about it. When he took us for our first dance, it surprised me how light he was on his feet. He remembered all those waltzes and foxtrots from a long time ago. As we danced I saw our reflection in a mirror and he smiled and said, "Now you look like my tie." I was sixteen and tiny beside him. At my seventeenth birthday party we had to water the gin.

When he began drinking I would just get lost, that was easy to do at Rock Hill. He'd be insensible; and then, when he was getting better, he was like an angel and would do anything for you. . . . There was a song he used to sing when he was drunk, over and over. He had made it up and he sang it only when he was really drunk. Partly English and partly Sinhalese, a bit like a baila as it used brand names and street names and gibberish. It made no sense to anyone but it wasn't gibberish to him because he always sang exactly the same words each time.

His last days were very quiet. He would allow himself one cigarette a day. After dinner he would go out onto the verandah and sit for about an hour by himself or with me before his radio programmes came on. He would have his cigarette then. If I wanted permission to do something such as go for a dance I would ask him then, for at that moment he was most content with things. I remember there was quite a ceremony of course. I would bring him the round tin of cigarettes and the matches and he would light one and smoke it slowly. That would be around 8 o'clock in the evening.

* * *

V. C. de Silva:

He was brilliant at selling chickens. I don't know how he did it, but he would put on this official air and that helped. If I could get 15 rupees for a pullet, he would get 27.50. But there was a certain amount of gullibility in his dealings with adults and some abused his generosity. When he had money he would spend it.

I was considered one of his closest friends. I was also his medical adviser, and we talked poultry and dogs. After your mother left in 1947, I lived with your father for a month. I was the go-between, taking flowers to your mother in Colombo. Then in 1950 I was practicing in Kandy and he came to see me because he was vomiting blood. Then he and I and Archer Jayawardene became close friends. We would meet once a week at the *Daily News* bookshop in Kandy.

We never drank with him. If Archer and I arrived at Rock Hill he would give us a large glass of ice-cold milk. He would always be reading my medical books, my dog and poultry books; he would brood on these things. When he had the D.T.'s I would give him half a grain of morphine to sedate him for 12 hours and he would come out of it ok. Before he died there was a second bout of haemorrhaging — stomach this time. But death was due to a cerebral haemorrhage.

There were just two or three of us who were very close to him. As for Maureen, I think she knew I was too close a friend for her to like me. God, I learned a great deal from him. There was nothing about poultry he didn't know. Or dogs. He used to have a lot of faith in me so I loved him too.

✳   ✳   ✳

Archer Jayawardene:

He was a founder of the Cactus and Succulent Society. We had a hundred members and once a year we would have lunch and tea at the Kandy Garden Club.

He loved organizing us. He suddenly decided to get us to dance in our old age. I think Maureen wanted to go to a New Year's Dance and he suggested that we all take dancing lessons. He hired a teacher and we had to take lessons twice a week. He was wonderful at planning these things — picnics, trips to the Perahera.

He loved the Perahera and always got into trouble during them. Once he ran over a policeman's foot. At the police station he fell asleep on the Inspector's desk and it took several men to move him.

But he spent most of his spare time reading or listening to that huge wireless on the front porch. He lived in another world I think. He was not interested in politics. Usually he never spoke about the past. But when the *coup* case was on he went down to Colombo to visit his old friends, Derek and Royce, in jail.

A year before he died he went into that terrible depression. V.C. de Silva and I would go there and he wouldn't speak to us. We were his closest friends and he ignored us. Just sat there completely still as if caught against something so he couldn't move. A cousin of mine was a psychiatrist and I drove him up from Colombo and I introduced him and before I had even stepped off the porch he was having a *hell* of a chat with that doctor.

His funeral was a tragi-comedy sort of business. First of all the coffin they brought was too small so they had to build a new one in the house. Then they couldn't get it out so they had to break the doors down. And the day of the funeral was a rainy day. He had bought this plot of land right at the top of a hill. We made that steep climb, carrying the coffin, slipping and falling to our knees on a thin muddy road.

He had not been well during that last year after the depression. He was content though. I think that both of us were impatient men. But the cactus and the gardening — you know — we had taught ourselves something. Now my wife and I have moved to this small house and the furniture still hasn't arrived, but I don't really care. The Buddhists say if you have things you only worry about them. I go cycling at three in the morning when the streets are empty . . . I'm really enjoying myself. I keep telling my wife we should get ready for the other life, the flying.

Two days before he died we were together. We were alone in the house. I can't remember what we said but we sat there for three hours. I too don't talk much. You know it is a most relaxed thing when you sit with a best friend and you know there is nothing you have to tell him, to empty your mind. We just stayed there together, silent in the dusk like this, and we were quite happy.

* * *

He would swing wildly, in those last years — not so much from sobriety to drink but from calmness to depression. But he was shy, he didn't want anyone else to be troubled by it, so he would be quiet most of the time. That was his only defense. To keep it within so the fear would not hurt others.

I keep thinking of the lines from Goethe . . . "Oh, who will heal the sufferings / Of the man whose balm turned poison?" I can only clarify this range in him by focussing on this metamorphosis. At the end he moved courteous among his few friends so they never realized, or could only guess at, his torn state, and by then he had already gone too far, was on the cliff. And how could his children know when he would write them his strange quirky notes, such as, "Dear Jenny — I am in the quite well. I hope you are in the same well. Love Daddy xxx"?

His fantasies were awful. Paranoia took over during his downward swings. He personally shattered three hundred eggs. Dug a pit and threw them in beating them to pieces with a large staff so nothing would survive — all because he knew someone was trying to poison the family. This he did secretly so no one would worry.

When he could no longer hold all the information, the awareness of what was happening, he would turn to drink. Or, in the last year before he died, he broke down completely. Ceremonies darkened around him. His two closest friends were saddened, not just for what had happened to him but because it seemed he no longer trusted them. He was in the well of total silence. Sat on the verandah looking out onto coconut trees, the suspect chickens. He cooked himself an omelette and a cup of soup. At this point he did not drink. He sat catatonic, his eyes drifting over the lawn. It was too late to act secure, polite.

They found a doctor he would talk to and he was taken to a nursing home in Colombo. When the children came to visit him he was distant with them because he thought they were imitations. He longed to hold his children in his arms. You must understand all this was happening while his first family was in England or Canada or Colombo totally unaware of what was happening to him. That would always be the curse on us, the guilt we would be left with.

He came home after two weeks cheerful and positive. Years earlier, Archer and Doreen Jayawardene had mentioned to him that Rock Hill was a "see devi" place, meaning a home of contentment and peace. Now when he saw them again he said, "Isn't this a see devi place once more?" And for the first time he explained to his friends the state of his darkness:

When I saw you come (my father said), I saw poisonous gas around you. You walked across the lawn to me and you were wading through green gas as if you were crossing a river by foot and you were not aware of it. And I thought if I speak, if I point it out it will destroy you instantly. I was immune. It would not kill me but if I revealed this world to you you would suffer for you had no knowledge, no defenses against it. . . .

About a year later he delivered some eggs to the railway station and on the way back decided to visit his cousin Phyllis in Kandy. She remembers him driving in while she sat on the porch and she stood up. He waved but kept on going round the circle of driveway and left, still waving. An hour later she received a phone call from him. He said, "You must have thought me quite mad, but I realized as I was slowing down that I was getting a flat tire so I felt I should get home quickly." They laughed cheerfully at the incident and those were the last words they spoke to each other.

There is so much to know and we can only guess. Guess around him. To know him from these stray actions I am told about by those who loved him. And yet, he is still one of those books we long to read whose pages remain uncut. We are still unwise. It is not that he became too complicated but that he had reduced himself to a few things around him and he gave them immense meaning and significance. The behaviour of certain creatures he could theorize on for hours with V.C. de Silva. He kept journals about every one of the four hundred varieties of cactus and succulents — some of which he had never seen, others of which he had smuggled into the country via a friend. Important days were those when certain waterplants arrived from islands in the Pacific. He had come to love the specific variety of growing things and the information he was taught by them. There were the invented games with his children. There was the relearning of old songs from the past to delight them. They could be charmed by the silliness of lyrics from the thirties which had always moved him.

Courtesy. A modesty. In spite of the excess of his gestures earlier in his life he was in the end a miniaturist pleased by small things, the decent gestures among a small circle of family and friends. He made up lovely songs about every dog he had owned — each of them had a different tune and in the verses he celebrated their natures.

"You must get this book right," my brother tells me, "You can only write it once." But the book again is incomplete. In the end all your children move among the scattered acts and memories with no more clues. Not that we ever thought we would be able to fully understand you. Love is often enough, towards your stadium of small things. Whatever brought you solace we would have applauded. Whatever controlled the fear we all share we would have embraced. That could only be dealt with one day at a time — with that song we cannot translate, or the dusty green of the cactus you touch and turn carefully like a wounded child towards the sun, or the cigarettes you light.

LAST MORNING

Half an hour before light I am woken by the sound of rain. Rain on wall, coconut, and petal. This sound above the noise of the fan. The world already awake in the darkness beyond the barred windows as I get up and stand here, waiting for the last morning.

My body must remember everything, this brief insect bite, smell of wet fruit, the slow snail light, rain, rain, and underneath the hint of colours a sound of furious wet birds whose range of mimicry includes what one imagines to be large beasts, trains, burning electricity. Dark trees, the mildewed garden wall, the slow air pinned down by rain. Above me the fan's continual dazzling of its hand. When I turn on the light, the bulb on the long three-foot cord will sway to the electrical breeze making my shadow move back and forth on the wall.

But I do not turn on the light yet. I want this emptiness of a dark room where I listen and wait. There is nothing in this view that could not be a hundred years old, that might not have been here when I left Ceylon at the age of eleven. My mother looks out of her Colombo window thinking of divorce, my father wakes after three days of alcohol, his body hardly able to move from the stiffness in muscles he cannot remember exerting. It is a morning scenery well known to my sister and her children who leave for swimming practice before dawn crossing the empty city in the Volks, passing the pockets of open shops and their lightbulb light that sell newspapers and food. I stood like this in the long mornings of my childhood unable to bear the wait till full daylight when I could go and visit the Peiris family down the road in Boralesgamuwa; the wonderful, long days I spent there with Paul and Lionel and Aunt Peggy who would casually object to my climbing all over her bookcases in my naked and dirty feet. Bookcases I stood under again this week which were full of signed first editions of poems by Neruda and Lawrence and George Keyt. All this was here before I dreamed of getting married, having children, wanting to write.

Here where some ants as small as microdots bite and feel themselves being lifted by the swelling five times as large as their bodies. Rising on their own poison. Here where the cassette now starts up in the next room. During the monsoon, on my last morning, all this Beethoven and rain.

REX DANIEL   CLEMENTI-SMITH   J. EPHRAUMS   ..RUEBORG   LILIAN DANIEL   EILEEN COOKE   G. PERAERA

MISS COOKE.   HARRY WENDT.   MISS VAN ROOYAN.   NITA DIAS

Doris Gratiaen's Dance, January 7, 1928

SHELTON DE SARAM

M. H.G. RATNAM   M. S. STANLEY DE SARAM   VERNA LOOS   TREVOR DE SARAM   CISSY DE SARAM   M. MARY ANTHONISZ.

S. ONKLAAS   PHYLLIS ONDAATJE   S. ONDAATJE   E. VAN LANGENBERG   FRED LEMBRUGGEN

ACKNOWLEDGMENTS

A literary work is a communal act. And this book could not have been *imagined*, let alone conceived, without the help of many people.

The book is a composite of two return journeys to Sri Lanka, in 1978 and 1980. On each occasion I stayed for several months, travelling alone and then joined by my wife and children. My sister, Gillian, took many of the journeys of research with me all over the island. She, and my other sister, Janet, and my brother, Christopher, were central in helping me recreate the era of my parents. This is their book as much as mine. My own family too had to put up with compulsive questioning of everyone we met, hearing again and again long lists of confused genealogies and rumour.

Raw material came from many sources; and I would like to thank a larger group of relatives, friends and colleagues who helped me in my inquisitiveness: Alwin Ratnayake, Phyllis and Ned Sansoni, Ernest and Nalini McIntyre, Zillah Gratiaen, Pam Fernando, Wendy

Partridge, Dolly van Langenberg, Susan and Sunil Perera, Jennifer Saravanamuttu, Archer and Doreen Jayawardene, V.C. de Silva, Peggy and Harold Peiris, Sylvia Fernando, Stanley Suraweera, Hamish and Gill Sproule, Dhama Jagoda, Ian Goonetileke, Yasmine Gooneratne, Wimal Dissanayake, Jilska Vanderwall, Rex and Bertha Daniels, Irene Vanderwall, Rohan and Kamini de Soysa, Erica Perera, Clarence de Fonseka, Nesta Brohier, Nedra de Saram, Sam Kadirgamar, Dorothy Lowman, John Kotelawala, Irangenie "Chandi" Meedeniya, Barbara Sansoni, Trevor de Saram, Thea Wickramasuriya, Jenny Fonseka, Yolande Ilangakoon, Babe Jonklaas, Verna and Mary Vangeyzel, Audrey de Vos . . . and Shaan, Eggily, and Hetti Corea.

While all these names may give an air of authenticity, I must confess that the book is not a history but a portrait or "gesture." And if those listed above disapprove of the fictional air I apologize and can only say that in Sri Lanka a well-told lie is worth a thousand facts.

*   *   *

Thanks to the Canada Council and Ontario Arts Council and Glendon College, York University, for their support. And to the editors of *The Capilano Review*, *periodics*, *The Canadian Forum*, and *Brick*, who published sections from the work in progress.

*   *   *

Finally, special thanks to three friends who helped me at many stages with the manuscript: Daphne Marlatt, Stan Dragland, and Barrie Nichol, *"for my papers ware promiscuous and out of forme with severall inlargements and untutored narrative."*

Credits

The stanza from the poem, "Don't Talk to Me about Matisse," comes from the book *O Regal Blood* by Lakdasa Wikkramaisinha, published in Colombo in February 1975.

The lines from Goethe are from a translation by James Wright in his *Collected Poems*. Published by Wesleyan University Press, 1971.

"Sea of Heartbreak" by Don Gibson. Copyright MCMLX and MCMLXI by Shapiro, Berstein & Co., Inc., 10 East 53 Street, New York 10022. International Copyright Secured. All rights reserved. Used by permission.

"It's Been a Long, Long Time" by Sammy Cahn & Jule Styne, published by Cahn Music Company and Morley Music Company.

"A Fine Romance" by Dorothy Fields & Jerome Kern. Copyright © 1936 T. B. Harms Company (c/o The Welk Music Group, Santa Monica, CA 90401) Copyright renewed. International Copyright Secured. All rights reserved. Used by permission.

The lines quoted in *The Karapothas* sequence linking Robinson Crusoe with Robert Knox's *An Historical Relation*, published by the Ceylon Historical Association.

The remarks by W. C. Ondaatje come from his "Report on the Royal Botanical Gardens, Peradeniya" which was published in Ceylon Almanac of 1853.

An excerpt from Rex Daniels' journal is used with his kind permission.

Photograph of the 1947 Nuwara Eliya flood courtesy of Dr Wickrema Weerasooriya.

Photograph of Sensation Rock from Cave's *Book of Ceylon*.

Every effort has been made to secure clearance for material used within this book.

MICHAEL ONDAATJE is the author of the internationally cele-brated novels *In the Skin of a Lion*, *The English Patient*, *Anil's Ghost* and *Divisadero*. His most recent novel is *The Cat's Table*. His other acclaimed and well-loved books of fiction and poetry include *Coming Through Slaughter*, *The Cinnamon Peeler*, *Handwriting* and *The Conversations: Walter Murch and the Art of Editing Film*. Michael Ondaatje was born in Ceylon (now Sri Lanka), and came to Canada in 1962. He lives in Toronto.